THE CHANGING FACE OF
GOLDEN

SPONSORED BY

The Golden Civic Foundation

GOLDEN CIVIC
FOUNDATION

Building a better Golden.

THE
DONNING COMPANY
PUBLISHERS

THE CHANGING FACE OF

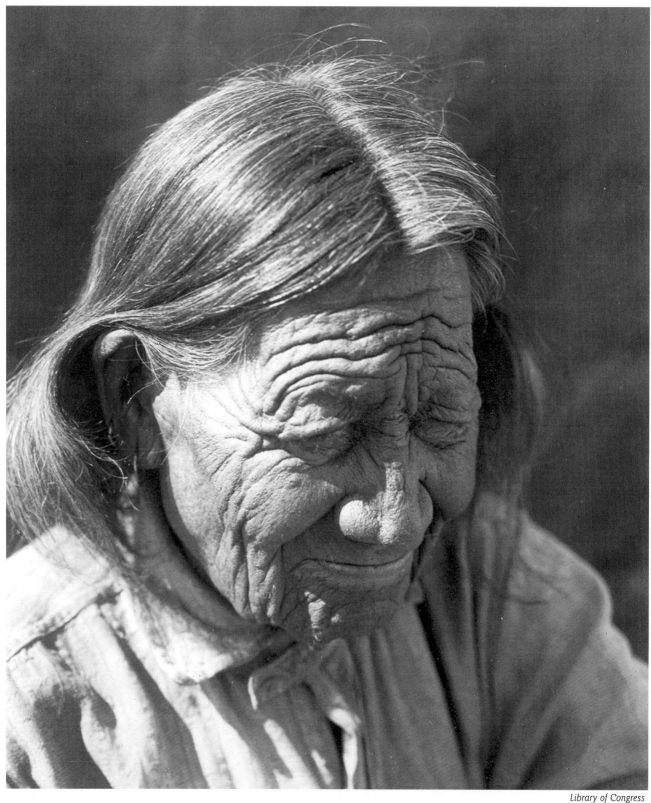

GOLDEN

By
Michelle L. Zupan and
Elinor E. Packard
Modern Photographs by Dave Shrum

The Donning Company Publishers
184 Business Park Drive, Suite 206
Virginia Beach, Virginia 23462-6533

Steve Mull, General Manager
Barbara Buchanan, Office Manager
Kathleen Sheridan, Senior Editor
Amanda Guilmain, Graphic Designer
Mary Ellen Wheeler, Proofreader/Editorial Assistant
Amanda Guilmain, Imaging Artist
Scott Rule, Director of Marketing
Travis Gallup, Marketing Coordinator
Anne Cordray, Project Research Coordinator

Barbara Bolton, Project Director

Library of Congress Cataloging-in-Publication Data

Zupan, Michelle L.
The changing face of Golden / by Michelle L. Zupan and Elinor E. Packard ; photographs by Dave Shrum.

p. cm.

ISBN 1-57864-278-7

1. Golden (Colo.)—Civilization. 2. Golden (Colo.)—Pictorial works. 3. Golden (Colo.)—Economic conditions. 4. Business enterprises—Colorado—Golden. I. Packard, Elinor E. II. Title.

F784.G57Z87 2004
978.8'84–dc22
2004014960

Contents

Introduction

The City of Golden, Colorado, is situated between the Great Plains and the foothills of the Rocky Mountains in a scenic valley bordered on the east by two imposing mesas and mountains to the west. First inhabited by the Native Americans as a seasonal hunting ground and later as the seat for one of Colorado's oldest counties, Golden has a long and rich history populated by colorful characters, unique events, discoveries and inventions that have shaped the world, and unique and interesting people who continue to leave an indelible impression on American society.

This history of the Golden region begins millions of years ago when volcanic activity, plate tectonics, and other immutable forces created the gold and silver deposits to the valley's west, when beds of coal and clay were laid down layer up on layer, awaiting the moment when they would be discovered and mined. Had it not been for the presence of those much needed and sought after resources, Colorado and Golden with it would have not been established until much later. There is little mining that occurs in Golden these days, but the vestiges remain in the form of place names and altered landscapes. White Ash Park commemorates the coal mine that once bore the name. Today, the jagged areas created by clay mines are covered over by gently rolling putting greens.

Clear Creek made Golden an opportune place for farming and ranching. Indeed, agriculture was the first money-making endeavor pursued in Golden to great success. David Wall realized $2,000 in profits from his first vegetable crop. While some livestock is still maintained near Golden, farming has gone by the wayside. However, the people who operated some of the most successful truck gardens have left their names as a permanent reminder. Street names such as Easley, Tripp, and Boyd remind modern residents of inhabitants past.

Economic depressions and political activities took their toll on Golden. As in any small town, remaining viable and relevant has always been a challenge for Golden's merchants. Competition from Denver and nearby cities is ever present. The Prohibition Amendment could have meant economic ruin for the town, but thanks to the creative endeavors of Adolph Coors and other town boosters, Golden survived.

Welcoming visitors since 1949, the Golden Arch was given to the City of Golden by Lu and Ethel Holland. Though the arch has undergone a variety of renovations since its installation, it has been placed on the State Register of Historic Places.

Throughout the years of the Colorado gold and silver booms, Golden served as the gateway to the mining districts. Railcars filled with all the wealth of the mountains flowed through the heart of the little town. Businesses of all types, including smelters, brick yards, flour mills, churches, and, of course, saloons, sprang up to meet the needs of the thousands of fortune-seekers and their families.

Historically, Golden's face has transfigured from one of the vast open plains from a seascape to a swampy quagmire, a veritable volcanic hot spot, back to a vast open plain, and finally to the bustling city we know today. It hasn't always been an easy transition. Indeed, Golden has been often fraught with obstacles and occasionally has come near extinction. Nevertheless, today, the valley situated between the mesas and the mountains and the city it shelters yet thrive. Bayard Taylor, a journalist visiting the region in 1866 on behalf of the *New York Tribune*, wrote of his impressions of Golden City:

> *The quiet of Golden City will not endure much longer; and the day may*
> *not be far off when the smokes from its tall chimneys, rising up behind*
> *Table Mountain, will be seen at Denver. (Taylor, 1889)*

Taylor's vision never came to pass. Golden never grew to the proportions many of its original founders and visitors envisioned. In some ways, Golden is still very much the way it was a century ago. Many of the vistas have not changed. Many of the issues absorbing the populace today are similar to those at the turn of the last century. However, as is true everywhere, man has left his indelible mark upon the landscape. History marches on and with it often go the people, structures, and ideas that were once held dear. This journey through Golden's five hundred-million-year history is not meant to be all-encompassing nor all-inclusive. Rather, it is a series of snapshots, brief sojourns to times and places past, and glimpses of what Golden is today.

The face Golden has shown the world has often been that of grit-and-guts. In the twenty-first century, this is no different. The town and its people have sometimes struggled to survive and change with the times. While the face of Golden is more modern now, with paved roads and sidewalks, brick buildings, and cultural offerings by the dozens, the grit and guts are still very evident just below the surface of every face and every façade in the town "Where the West Lives."

In the 1970s, the arch's motto was changed to "Where the West Lives"; it often sports a banner announcing community events.

Acknowledgments

This project would simply not have been possible without the incredible cooperation and patience of many people.

Michelle and Elinor would like to extend their gratitude to the Golden Pioneer Museum Board of Directors, Ms. Sarah West for the jacket design, Ms. Brie Kelly, Mr. Chuck Hearn, Mr. Bob Sorgenfrei, Ms. Joan Howard, Ms. Leslie Olsen, Mr. Uldis Jansons, Mr. Jerry Ilgenfritz, Ms. Lorraine Wagenbach, Mr. Peter Ewers, staff of the Stephen Hart Library at the Colorado Historical Society, the staff at the Western History Department of the Denver Public Library, Kathy Husband and the many staff members of the Jefferson County Library District who all spent many hours assisting with locating obscure references and answering innumerable dumb questions, the patient staff of Colorado Camera, the *Golden Transcript*, the U.S. Department of Energy, the Golden Lions Club, the Golden Fortnightly Club, the Mount Lookout Chapter, NSDAR, the members of the Golden Cultural Alliance, Mr. William "Chip" Parfet, the Golden Volunteer Fire Department, and the Golden Police Department for all their assistance in gathering information, posing for photographs, and providing moral support. Michelle and Elinor also extend a very special thank you to those members of the Golden community who offered tremendous support and encouragement. If we have inadvertently omitted anyone, we accept full responsibility, and our sincere apology and also our sincere thank you.

The Changing Face of Golden is a collection of entertaining anecdotes from many sources; it is not a definitive history of Golden. It is meant to document Golden's similarities and differences throughout its fascinating history and into the present.

View from South Table Mountain ca. 1875

Chapter One 1

**An Uplifting Experience: The
Geology and Geography of Golden**

View from South Table Mountain, 2003.

The current history of the Golden region is one that doesn't begin 150 years ago with the Gold Rush or 12,000 years ago with the arrival of the first Native Americans or even 65 million years ago with the rumbling steps of the mega lizards that populated the Front Range. Its history more appropriately begins about 500 million years ago when the Denver Basin, in which Golden sits, began to sink and the Ancestral Rocky Mountains began to form.

Geographically, Golden, Colorado, is situated, at 105° W longitude and 40° N latitude. It is and always has been the county seat of Jefferson County, one of the state's oldest counties. The town is more than a mile above sea level, cozily ensconced between the soaring Central Rocky Mountains to the west and the cliffs of the mesas of North and South Table Mountains to the east. Clear Creek, a tributary to the South Platte River, divides the town into distinct north and south sections. Like most of Colorado, the town enjoys nearly 300 days of sunshine and averages about thirteen inches of precipitation annually.

EON	ERA	PERIOD	
Phanerozoic Eon	Cenozoic Era "Age of Mammals" 65 mya through today	Quaternary Period "The Age of Man" 1.8 mya to today	
		Tertiary Period 65 to 1.8 mya	Neogene 24-1.8 mya
			Paleogene 65-24 mya
"Visible Life" Organisms with skeletons or hard shells. 540 mya through today	Mesozoic Era "Age of Reptiles" 248 to 65 mya	Cretaceous Period 146 to 65 mya	
		Jurassic Period 208 to 146 mya	
		Triassic Period 248 to 208 mya	
	Paleozoic Era 540 to 248 mya	Permian Period "Age of Amphibians" 290 to 248 mya	
		Carboniferous 360 to 290 mya	325 to 290 mya
			360 to 325 mya
		Devonian Period "The Age of Fishes" 408 to 360 mya	
		Silurian Period, 438 to 408 mya	
		Ordovician Period, 505 to 438 mya	
		Cambrian Period, 540 to 500 mya	
2.5 billion years ago to 540 mya		600 to 540 mya	
Archeozoic Eon (Archean) 3.9 to 2.5 billion years ago			
Hadean Eon 4.6 to 3.9 billion years ago			

Geologic timetable. Courtesy: U.S. Geological Survey.

The topography around Golden consists of gently rolling hills, traditionally covered with native grass species such as blue grama and buffalo grass. Prior to continuous human occupation, pronghorn antelope, mule deer, elk, coyote, mountain lion, and myriad other species inhabited the valley. Today, a semiresident elk herd roams the golf course, deer nibble at carefully planted petunias, the plaintive songs of the coyote often waft from the tops of North Table Mountain, and the occasional bear or mountain lion meanders through a neighborhood.

Red rock formations near Morrison, Colorado ca. 1880.

An Uplifting Experience

On the geologic time scale, 500 million years ago is but a drop in the bucket in the grand scheme of earth and human existence, but it is a worthy spot to begin the journey through Golden's

Red Rocks Park, 2003.

past. At that time, most of what would become the western portion of the United States was a vast plain, a home to plants and animals. Then the Denver Basin began to subside, giving rise to a mountain range that would exist for the next 200 million years—the Ancestral Rockies. Remnants of this massive range are still evident throughout the area, including Mount Morrison.

As the mountains eroded, various animals left evidence of their lives in the region. The fossil remains of scorpionlike arthropods, predinosaurians, amphibians, and insects are found in rock deposits of the old Fountain Formation. The dramatic red sandstone formations at Red Rocks Park, south of Golden, date to this period. Nearly 280 million years ago, sand dunes were the dominant feature of the area, covered with conifers and inhabited by reptilelike mammals. Their remains are in the Lyons Sandstone found along the Front Range.

Volcanic cap rock, South Table, ca. 1860.

60 million-year-old dinosaur tracks near Mount Morrison, ca. 1940.

About 200 million years before present, the climate was somewhat warmer and wetter. The Lykins Formation is a red mudstone indicative of a tropical mudflat. The area would have not been conducive to habitation, so evidence of life is slight except for the occasional stromatolite.

At about 150 million years ago, the earth began to shake. Inhabiting the plains of Colorado were the first of the large plant-eating dinosaurs, including the Apatosaurus. Tracks of these immense beasts can be viewed south of Golden on the west side of Dinosaur Ridge. The tracks date to the Jurassic Age, when conifer forests hedged a floodplain dotted with lakes. By 100 million years ago, an inland sea had crept into the area. It was quite shallow, and Golden was on the very edge of it. The sea lasted until about 65 million years ago. Arthur Lakes, a noted geologist of the 1800s, discovered fossils of Pterosaurs, a flying dinosaur, and Mosasaurs, a huge prehistoric fish, near the town of Morrison, just south of Golden, in rocks dating to 65 million years ago. On land, Tyrannosaurus Rex and Triceratops may have battled for space in the mangrove swamps. Fossils of these beasts have been found on South Table Mountain. Tracks of many species of dinosaur are found throughout the Front Range, indicating that the shoreline may have been a migration route for many species of animals.

The dinosaur tracks are now maintained and interpreted by the Friends of Dinosaur Ridge, 2003.

Eventually the sea retreated, and the dinosaurs succumbed to the perils of evolution. About 65 million years ago, The area that is now Colorado began to blow its top. For the next 30 million years, volcanic activity reached its peak in the area. The volcanic caps of both North and South Table Mountains were formed at this time by a now extinct volcanic flow. Neither of the mesas is a volcano; geologists believe the flows came from vents or fissures to the northwest of North Table Mountain. Three distinct flows contributed to the impressive formations visible today including Castle Rock, looming high over east Golden.

Arthur Lakes, artist and geologist, often rendered his excavation sites in watercolor. Courtesy: Peabody Museum, Yale University.

F. E. Everett.

Mammals and palm trees inhabited the Front Range. At about 60 million years ago, the land began to rumble once again, this time from deep inside the earth. The present-day Rocky Mountain Range was born when the Pacific Plate crashed into the North American Plate at the present-day San Andreas Fault in California. The faulting or wrinkling of the land produced the present day Rockies. Today's 11,000 to 14,000-foot peaks, presumed to have been in excess of 20,000 feet in height when first formed, are still impressive.

Much of what we know about Golden's geologic past comes from work begun in the 1870s by Arthur Lakes. In 1869, Lakes, considered by many scientists the "Father of Colorado Geology," began teaching at Jarvis Hall, an Episcopal school. He continued teaching when the school was turned over to the Territorial Government for the State School of Mines.

Lakes, an itinerant deacon for the Episcopal Church, discovered some vertebrate fossils near the town of

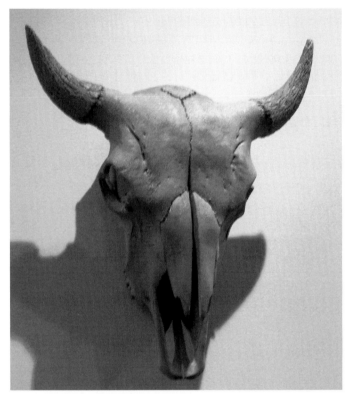

Skull of a Plains buffalo (Bison bison).

Palm frond impression at Fossil Trace Golf Course.

Morrison. He and colleague Henry Beckwith began excavating throughout spring and summer 1877, finding fossils from Apatosaurus, Diplodocus, and Stegosaurus, though at the time these species had not been previously recognized. Lakes immediately contacted Yale University's Professor O. C. Marsh. Marsh identified one of the species as being entirely new and named it Titanosaurus montanus, later to be reclassified as Apatosaurus.

Lakes' excavations so fascinated and confounded area residents that many became certain the entire hogback, or ridged mountain, where the men were excavating must certainly be the petrified remains of some gigantic monster. In all, Lakes excavated some ten separate quarries near Morrison. The Stegosaurus was eventually named Colorado's state fossil.

Engineer and surveyor Edward Berthoud found Lakes' discoveries so fascinating that he made mention of them in his *History of Jefferson County*, telling how teeth from a sixty-foot-long Megalosaur had been discovered near Golden as well. Berthoud also notes the discoveries of the teeth of elephant and mastodon and elephant tusks (probably mammoth) nearby. Golden banker F. E. Everett discovered a bison skull on his land just outside of town.

The Louisiana Purchase of 1803. From: Newhouse, 1992.

Today, visitors can view the fruition of Lakes' work. While all his excavated fossils were shipped to the Yale Peabody Museum in Connecticut, more recent excavations have located footprints, fossils, and ripple marks all along the hogbacks between Golden and Morrison. Dinosaur Ridge is the single best location to view tens of millions of years of prehistory. The Dinosaur Ridge Museum and walking tour showcase some of these remarkable finds.

Golden's rich fossil finds are not to be forgotten, however. One of the newest additions to the town's landscape is the Fossil Trace Golf Course. The course derived its moniker from the myriad prehistoric remains that grace its eighteen fairways. Since the 1800s, various geology and mining journals have recorded the footprints and plant impressions that now grace the vertical outcrops on the golf course. The sandstone outcrops bear impressions of palm fronds, dinosaur footprints, and various other interesting pieces of the ancient past. These are on permanent exhibit for the intrepid golfer willing to land a drive amidst the remains of the earth shakers of long ago.

Europe Discovers America

At the time the first Americans in the Golden area arrived about 12,000 years ago, North America was in the depths of an Ice Age. Vast sheets of ice covered much of the northern reaches of the continent. Mega-fauna such as mammoths and mastodons roamed the corridors between the ice sheets. Ice Age hunters followed the herds much later. By the fifteenth century, America had new visitors to its shores. The next snapshot in Golden's album is the evolution of Colorado as a part of the United States. It was neither a quick nor easy transition.

Spain was the first European country to lay claim to this portion of the world. Her claim on North America began with Christopher Columbus' arrival in 1492. The French and British followed suit and laid claim to portions of North America, but the majority of western North America was still under the Spanish flag. By and large, the Spanish were not very interested in the northernmost reaches of their land claim. A few isolated explorations had been made to search for mineral wealth, specifically gold, but little had proven worthy of further examination.

In 1682, the French extended their claim to include the land from the Allegheny to the Rocky Mountains. For the subsequent eighty years, the area was traversed by French-Canadian trappers. In a 1762 treaty, France returned the land to Spain. The 1763 Treaty of Paris, ending the Seven Years War between France and England, ceded Canada to France, and the land east of the Mississippi River to Great Britain. The treaty also ratified the land that France ceded to Spain in 1762. Following the American Revolution, the Second Treaty of Paris transferred the land east of the Mississippi River to the United States. The western lands remained under Spanish control.

In the 1801 Treaty of Madrid, a remarkably clandestine arrangement, Spain returned Louisiana and control of most of the land west of the Mississippi River Valley to France. French control of such a major waterway was extraordinarily problematic for the United States. The French would not permit United States access to the Port of New Orleans, thereby severing commerce with towns upriver such as St. Louis. President Thomas Jefferson and his Cabinet began making overtures to Napoleon's government for the purchase of New Orleans. In yet another low-key agreement, Napoleon's representative sold to the United States not only New Orleans but also the entirety of France's western holdings north to the present Canadian border for three cents per acre. The 1803 Louisiana Purchase included the future states of Louisiana, Arkansas, Missouri, Kansas, Nebraska, Iowa, South Dakota, North Dakota, and most of the states of Montana, Wyoming, and Oklahoma plus one-third of Colorado. The remainder of what would become

"The Accurate Map of North America from the Latest Discoveries," ca.1750–89. Map shows colonies, some cities and towns, and Indian tribal territories.

Explorer Major Stephen H. Long, ca. 1840.

Colorado, Wyoming, and New Mexico was purchased from the Republic of Texas in 1850 following the Mexican War.

The French believed the area possessed great mineral wealth. However, it was so foreboding that few but the most adventurous Europeans had risked travels in the area. Immediately after the Louisiana Purchase, the U.S. government commissioned scientific exploration of the territory to see what it had bought. Meriwether Lewis and William Clark had the distinction of being the first American explorers to traverse the entire breadth of the new lands. They did not, however, venture into Colorado.

Lieutenant Zebulon Pike's 1806 expedition took him to the foot of the Rocky Mountains. So dismayed was he by the vast plains that he dubbed the area the "Great American Desert."

Mr. and Mrs. Rufus Sage.

It wasn't until Major Stephen Long and his party visited the region in 1820 that the image of a "vast desert" was somewhat dispelled. Long wrote eloquent accounts of the abundance of the area, which he found quite picturesque. On July 5, members of Long's party traversed the area of Cannonball Creek—present-day Clear Creek—where they purported to have shot a pronghorn antelope for dinner. John R. Bell, traveling with the party, recorded these notes in his journal:

> This creek is rapid and clear, flowing over a bed paved with rounded masses of granite-gneiss. It is from a supposed resemblance to these masses to cannon balls that the creek has received its name from the French hunters. The channel is sunk from fifty to one hundred feet below the common level of the plains.

Itinerant trappers and traders made their way through Colorado, occasionally making mention of the Clear Creek valley. Louis Vasquez, the French-Canadian trader, traversed the valley in 1832 seeking a location for his new trading post. He didn't choose the valley but left a lasting memory of himself by renaming Cannonball Creek Vasquez Fork. The next recorded visitor was Rufus Sage, who was on a voyage of discovery, mostly for himself. During fall and winter 1843, he camped along the Vasquez Fork, as Clear Creek was known then. His notes on the valley, published in *Scenes in the Rocky Mountains and in Oregon, New Mexico, Texas, and the Grand Prairies*, include mentions that the area was well timbered, had good soil, abundant clay stone, excellent gravels, and sufficient deer, elk, and mountain sheep. Sage also conducted some placer mining (gold panning), recovering some gold, but did not feel it worthy of promoting further. Thus, Colorado remained unnoticed by most of the eastern United States.

Gold panner in the Colorado Territory. Courtesy Summit County Historical Society.

Chapter Two

**Between the Mountains and the Plains:
The First People**

Cheyenne village, Colorado Territory, 1860. From Crofutt, 1885.

The first people to set sight on the Golden area arrived approximately 12,000 years ago. They came on foot, bundled into hooded fur parkas, carrying their belongings in animal hide packs. They followed herds of game across the Bering Land Bridge and sailed in small boats along the coastal marshes from Asia to the unexplored land to the east. These nomadic explorers found an open prairie situated between large sheets of glacial ice, haven to large mammals such as mammoth, ground sloth, and three-toed horse. It was a hunter's paradise. What those early immigrants called themselves will be forever lost to prehistory, but we do know the area that is now Colorado enjoyed the distinction of being a relatively ice-free corridor for people and animals to pass through. The climate would have been colder than present day but not enough to deter habitation. The early hunters, called Paleo-Indians by archaeologists, were nomadic, traveling from site to site, following the animals on their seasonal migrations. We now know these people as Native Americans.

A scraper and projectile points from the Magic Mountain archaeological site.

Clovis culture, named for the location in New Mexico where it was first identified, is considered the first of these cultural groups to traverse the Americas. The term does not refer to a specific group of people but rather the common elements of culture that they shared. By and large, the

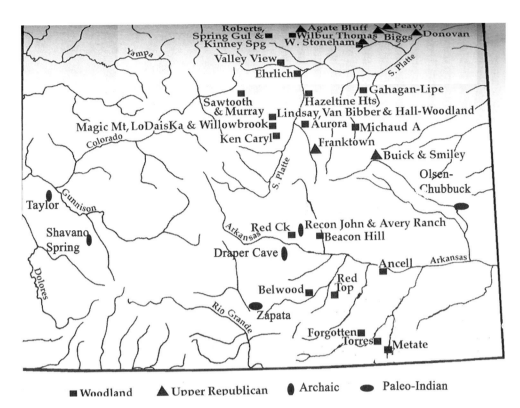

Colorado archaeological sites. From Cassells, 1997.

■ Woodland ▲ Upper Republican ◗ Archaic ⬮ Paleo-Indian

Clovis people hunted large mammals as a preference, with smaller animals such as rabbits supplementing their diet. They generally utilized a special type of lanceolate-shaped stone projectile point about twelve inches long attached to a spear that was launched with the help of an atlatl, or wooden throwing stick.

At the end of the last Ice Age, as the mammoth died out the Clovis culture was giving way to the Folsom culture. The people were likely the same, but with new generations come new tool and food preferences. The Folsom hunters were still nomadic but this time chose a large species of bison for their preferred game. Compared with modern buffalo, *Bison antiquaas* was an immense species that the Folsom people hunted using a special type of fluted projectile point. These points ranged in size from just a few inches long to ten to twelve inches. A thin piece of stone was removed from each "face" of the point, running from the base to nearly the top of the point. Current theories hold that these flutes helped do two things: they made it easier to haft the point to a spear tip, and when the point penetrated an animal's body, the flute allowed the blood to flow out more quickly, thereby quickening the animal's demise. Whatever they were for, the points were extraordinarily difficult to make and were made for only about 1,000 years.

There is only one site near Golden that has been confirmed to be of Paleo-Indian origin. Within seventy miles to the east, north, and south of the city, there are sites that indicate the Paleo-Indian hunters were in the area and processing mammoth and bison for their meals. Among these sites are Lamb Springs in Littleton and Dent on the South Platte River.

Large mammals, the primary food source of the Paleo-Indians, were dying out 8,500 years ago, and the climate was becoming warmer and drier. With the change in diet came changes in Native

Magic Mountain excavation, 1996. Courtesy Centennial Archaeology.

technology. During the Archaic Period, people began to use more plant foods, evidenced by manos and metates appearing in their campsites. The flat or basin-shaped stone metate hold seeds, nuts, berries, or greens, which are ground up with a mano, or hand stone, for use in stews or in pemmican, an early-day survival food. The Native people were also hunting smaller animals such as rabbits, deer, and antelope, and their projectile points grew smaller as a result. A climatic shift to warmer, drier seasons appears to have forced inhabitants of the Plains to move into the cooler and wetter mountains.

Native Americans began spending more time in and around the Golden area during the Archaic Period. Campsites, possible drive lines, and kill sites abound in the area. Golden and the surrounding area offered

The Apache traversed the Colorado area prior to the arrival of Spanish explorers.

optimal amenities for short- and long-term residency with abundant food, both animal and vegetable; continual water supplies; high ridges for lookout posts; rock overhangs for shelter; and a relatively mild climate. Major sites in the area include LoDaisKa (state site #5JF142) and Magic Mountain (5JF223). Among the smaller sites are Hall-Woodland Cave (5JF9), Lindsay Ranch, and Van Bibber Creek. Magic Mountain has been excavated several times over the last century and has been placed on the National Register of Historic Places to help ensure its preservation, and LoDaisKa is being considered for addition. Both sites indicate a long and fascinating prehistory of Colorado's Native population.

About 2,000 years ago, at the beginning of the Plains Ceramic period, the bow and arrow and pottery appeared on the Plains. By and large, Plains groups were still largely nomadic, following herds of game and moving with the changing seasons. However, several unique sites such as Magic Mountain seem to indicate that some groups were spending longer periods in a single location. Rock shelters and even combination stone and brush dwellings appear to have been the habitations of choice.

Historic Tribes

The tribes that are known to have inhabited the area of present day Colorado didn't even arrive on the scene until about C.E. 1500. Most of what we know about these groups comes from the journals of French and Spanish explorers as well as those observations made by early trappers and traders who worked directly with the Native Americans. In 1540, Francisco Vasquez de Coronado made the first Spanish expedition to the Great Plains and claimed it all for the king of Spain. With the exception of converting the tribes to Christianity, the Spaniards were not concerned with Colorado's Native inhabitants. They traded with them openly, giving horses and guns for bison robes and beaver pelts. The French claimed the same land in 1682 by right of owning the Mississippi River Valley and all lands drained by it. The United States acquired the

Paraglider soaring off Hall Woodland Cave site.

Although there are many photographs of Native Americans taken during the nineteenth century, most were staged or taken in Eastern studios. There are no known photographs of Native Americans taken in the Golden area. Arapaho Indian. Photo by Edward S. Curtis.

Six tribal leaders, probably at Theodore Roosevelt's Inauguration, 1905. From left: Little Plume (Piegan), Buckskin Charley (Ute), Geronimo (Chiricahua Apache), Quanah Parker (Comanche), Hollow Horn Bear (Brulé Sioux), and American Horse (Oglala Sioux). Courtesy Library of Congress

lands west of the Mississippi River in a series of treaties and purchases beginning with the Louisiana Purchase.

With the arrival of the settlers from the eastern United States came the notion that something had to be done about the "Indian problem." Most of the eastern tribes had been eradicated by guns, disease, and removal to the West. Native Americans were considered expendable in the path of progress, and those in the West were about to become the next victims of this mindset.

By the late 1860s, easterners' eyes were opened to the plight of the Indians following events such as the Sand Creek Massacre in 1864. Eastern newspapers demanded more civil treatment for the tribes. Nevertheless, westerners maintained a fundamentally different view about the "poor Indian" (*Colorado Transcript*, July 1867). In reality, atrocities occurred on both sides. People settled in the West to escape population pressures, war, and a host of other ills in the East; the Indians were in their way. The Indians were seeking to retain the lands and to hang onto a lifestyle that was no longer viable in a changing world. Tensions rose, and conflict was inevitable.

Plains Indian artifacts.

Comanche

Among the first identifiable groups in Colorado were the Apache and the Navajo (Diné). Both of these tribes originated in Canada and moved through the Plains before settling in present-day New Mexico and Arizona. Spanish records indicate that the Jicarilla band of Apaches was still living in and around northeastern Colorado as late as the 1500s and were driven out by the arrival of the Kiowa and Comanche toward the end of that century.

The Comanche originated in the northern Plains and probably came to Colorado via the Great Basin of Utah. The tribe is thought to be related to the Shoshone and Ute because of similarities in language. The Comanche are first mentioned in Spanish records around 1706 in the context of horse trades. Being the first Plains tribe to acquire horses in trade, the Comanche used them most effectively. They became the most adept equestrians in the history of North America. Trick riding, fighting, and buffalo hunting were just a few of the uses for horses. The area around Golden would have provided excellent pasturage for their horse herds.

By the 1820s, the Comanche had moved south of the Arkansas River. They took their large horse herds with them and grew into legendary horse-mounted warriors. Settlers in Texas lived in fear of Comanches—including their leader, Tarantula—who were known to be fearless and openly

Dolls made by the Comanche tribe of Oklahoma ca. 1930.

Dolls made by the Kiowa tribe ca. 1930.

Kiowa Spiritualism

Kiowa religious beliefs were founded on the belief in sacred power, called medicine, contained within and exemplified by particular things such as hawks, buffalo, and wind. Tribal traditions are passed down through stories. Generally, the stories were told during the month of the Sun Dance, the Kiowa's major religious ceremony that ensured an adequate supply of buffalo and tribal well-being. Such stories could be told only during the summer and only by the Keepers of the Medicines.

One of the sacred stories explains the origins of the sacred medicine bundles. The Kiowa have ten tribal "medicines," called "boy medicines" or the "ten grandmothers." These medicines or sacred bundles originated with the Split Boys. According to legend, a woman married Sun Boy and bore his son. The woman died, and the child was raised by Spider Old Woman. The child was split in two; thus, the Split Boys. The twins experience a variety of adventures and vanquish many monsters. Eventually, one boy disappears into the water, and the other transforms himself into a sacred bundle or "medicine" that then divides into ten bundles.

Keepers are designated for the bundles. However, anyone may ask them for assistance. One stipulation is that no violence may take place in the presence of the bundles, so tipis, where the bundles were kept, became places of refuge. The keepers of the medicines would pass them along to their heirs. The heirs would also inherit certain powers and duties along with the bundles. One such duty was relating the story of the Split Boys.

hostile to settlers. Eventually, under a series of treaties, the Comanche were placed on reservation lands in Oklahoma along with the Kiowa and Apache, their nineteenth-century enemy.

Kiowa

Originating in Montana, the Kiowa (*KI-o-wah*) had moved into central Colorado by 1732. Being a small band, they soon became allies with the Comanche against the Apache and other tribes hostile to them. Like other tribes in the Americas, they used dogs to transport their possessions until acquisition of the horse. These dogs were reputed to be able to carry packs as heavy as one hundred pounds. When the Spanish arrived, the Kiowa were eager to trade buffalo hides for horses, which soon became integral to the Kiowa way of life.

Trade between tribes for food as well as personal items was a common activity. This Ute child carries a bag made by the Hopi of Arizona ca. 1880. Courtesy Library of Congress.

Never a large tribe, the Kiowa were hit especially hard by western expansionism. Disease took its fatal toll on many tribes, including the Kiowa. Among these diseases were smallpox, which the Kiowa called the "hole sickness," that killed one-third of a generation in any given outbreak. Every ten or so years from 1780 to 1850, outbreaks of cholera, called the "cramp sickness," and the measles, called the "pimple sickness," wiped out hundreds. Those spared by disease were often vulnerable to starvation or war. The Kiowa moved with the Comanche to Oklahoma in the 1860s.

Ute

The Ute (*yoot*) are a Shoshonean tribe that has inhabited the eastern Great Basin of Utah, the Colorado western slope, and the central mountains of Colorado for nearly 1,000 years. Precisely when they arrived is unknown, but they bear many cultural similarities to people who inhabited the caves and rock shelters of the region around A.D. 900. In the 1600s, the Spaniards wrote extensively of the Ute in their journals of westward exploration.

These nomadic people traveled from the high mountains to the low foothills in their annual cycles. They would summer in the mountains where it was cooler, then winter at lower elevations in rock shelters and caves. In addition, some bands used tipis or brush structures called wickiups for shelter. The Utes were known to be fierce warriors. They made frequent raids on neighboring tribes to steal women, children, food, and later, horses. The raids continued unabated until the middle of the nineteenth century when settlers in Utah and Colorado began homesteading the lands traditionally occupied by the Ute.

Based on early accounts from trappers, explorers, and the Utes themselves, their land extended from Golden on the east to North Park on the north, the Animas River on the south, and the Sevier Lake in Utah on the west—roughly 56 million acres in Colorado and 23.5 million acres in Utah. In 1868, the lands were reduced to 18 million acres in Colorado. This moved the bands to the western side of the Continental Divide. However, according to both the *Western Mountaineer* and the *Colorado Transcript*, the Ute continued to make forays into Golden for supplies and to occasionally raid the Arapaho.

2 Moons, Cheyenne Indian. Photograph by Edward S. Curtis. Courtesy Library of Congress.

During the 1880s, the Utes were engaged in the favorite pastime of horseracing. A confrontation at Milk Creek, Colorado, between Colorado militia soldiers and the Utes resulted in deaths on both sides. This prompted the Dawes Severalty Act of 1887, which removed the Utes in Colorado to 40,000 acres in the far southwestern corner of the state. Since that time, the land allotted to the Utes in Colorado has dropped to 5,000 acres.

Arapaho and Cheyenne

When people think of Plains tribes, the Arapaho and Cheyenne usually come to mind. They are romanticized in countless Western movies, sporting elaborate eagle feather war bonnets. But neither tribe originated on the Plains. The Arapaho are thought to be a subgroup of the Gros Ventre tribes of Canada. They are first mentioned in 1795 as the Caminanbiches, living along the Cheyenne River in what is now South Dakota. Their modern designation of Arapaho is probably related to a Pawnee word meaning "one who trades." Lewis and Clark called them the "blue bands." They call themselves the "hino no 'éíno", which means "our people."

This letter, dated September 1864, illustrates the fear and often misinformation that the early settlers possessed about the Native inhabitants of the area.

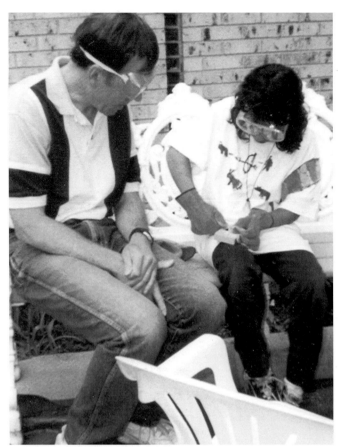

This participant in the Golden Pioneer Museum's Discover Archaeology Field School is learning the tradition of flint knapping.

The Cheyenne came from the Great Lakes area, where they lived in small villages, gathering wild rice and other plant foods, hunting waterfowl, and probably engaging in small-scale farming. As the East began to fill with people, new frontiers were opened in the wilderness, forcing the Cheyenne and other tribes farther west. Pressure from the Sioux and other eastern tribes pushed them west, bringing them to the Black Hills of South Dakota by the mid-1700s. There they acquired horses and took up a nomadic lifestyle, preferring to drag tipi poles from place to place and hunt buffalo, as Plains tribes had done for millennia. By the early nineteenth century, they had formed an alliance with the Arapaho and were wintering along the foothills of the Rocky Mountains. The word "Cheyenne" is probably from the Dakota word "Shahiyena," which means "people who talk differently." The Cheyenne's name for themselves is "Tsistsintas," or "Human Beings."

The two tribes remained bound by a similar language and culture. Eventually both groups would split into northern and southern bands. The southern bands still reside together in Oklahoma. It was this combined band of Southern Arapaho-Cheyenne that was living in the Golden area when settlers and gold seekers arrived.

In the early years of settlement, the Plains tribes were welcome additions to the frontier. They were skilled hunters and trappers and could assist the fur companies in their work to supply eastern stores with the hides they so craved. By the 1850s, the annual production of buffalo robes was right at 100,000. A Native American woman could process about twenty-five to thirty robes over the course of a winter. The Bent brothers, operating a trading post on the Arkansas River, invited the Southern Cheyenne to camp around their post and assist with the hunting.

At the time, very few emigrants from America were venturing across the "Great American Desert," encompassing Nebraska, Kansas, North and South Dakota, Colorado, Wyoming, Utah, and Nevada. From 1840 to 1848, only about 18,800 people made the overland crossing to reach the California gold fields. Presuming the Plains would never attract settlers, the Fort Laramie Treaty of 1851 designated the lands of Western Kansas Territory, Nebraska Territory, and South Dakota to be reservation lands for the Arapaho, Cheyenne, Crow, Teton Sioux, and Assiniboin.

That all changed with the discovery of gold in the western Kansas Territory in 1858. Knowing that a crossing of the Rocky Mountains was no longer necessary, emigrants came in droves to what would become the Colorado gold fields. In the next two years, about 100,000 people made the trip overland to the heart of Ute-Cheyenne-Arapaho territory. Almost immediately, the 1851 treaty was discarded in favor of the 1842 Preemption Act, which granted settlers 160 acres for the purchase price of $1.25 per acre. As most of the prospectors also sought a homestead, this was a golden deal.

Hostilities abounded between settlers and the Native Americans. Emigrants wrote home of their abject terror of being accosted by Indians. On January 6, 1859, Thomas Golden sent off the following note from the Arapahoe City settlement on Clear Creek, east of the present site of Golden:

The Indians are thick here. We apprehend danger from them. They have sent us word by some of their chiefs to quit the country, but we think we can stand them a rub, as we have 700 white men here.

During the Civil War, the Union and Confederate governments both sought assistance from the Native population. The Union wanted them to help protect the gold fields, while the Confederates used them as scouts and in raiding parties. However, the war was so far removed from the Territory that the hostile acts continued unabated. In 1864, the Colorado Territorial government was so concerned that the Cheyenne and Arapaho would declare war against the miners that it launched a preemptive strike in November on the combined tribes' reservation on the Big Sandy in southeastern Colorado. War was indeed declared after the Sand Creek Massacre, culminating in the defeat of Custer at Little Big Horn River. After that, all Plains tribes were confined to reservations scattered throughout the West.

As early as 1867, the Smithsonian Institution was aware that these unique cultures might not survive the hostilities. Through newspapers coast to coast, it issued a call for artifacts. The article appearing in the *Colorado Transcript* on June 12, 1867, announced that the Smithsonian was collecting specimens that illustrated the history of Native tribes from the earliest known period to the present. Among the items sought were photographic portraits, human crania (skulls), arrowheads, pipes, pottery, boats, and lodges. Collectors were admonished to provide accurate information as to when the item was procured, locality, date, Native name, and use. These collections residing within museum walls are the only remnants of some tribes that disappeared during the early days of settlement.

The Native American population declined dramatically in Colorado during the reservation period, from the 1870s through the 1920s. This decline may have been the origin of a Golden legend that the Arapaho would not venture into the valley because something bad had occurred there. The relative scarcity of Arapaho in the area after the 1864 Sand Creek Massacre would have made it appear the people were avoiding the area. However, accounts in the *Colorado Transcript* indicate that not only were the Arapaho regular visitors, but the Ute were as well. On occasion, the Arapaho would pass through the area on their way to a battle with their old enemies, the Ute. More often than not, at least until they were removed to reservations, the Native Americans were in town seeking food rations from the territorial governor. They would often camp for a few days, then disappear before dawn.

Fortunately, *Rocky Mountain News* founder William Byers was not quite correct in his estimation of the Native American situation in 1901:

> *Nevertheless, the fact remains that the aborigines of Colorado were an unknown people of an unknown age, who have left us naught but their bones, their implements of industry, their weapons of war, and their ruined habitations as the evidence of their existence.*

In recent years, the Native American presence has experienced a resurgence. Of Colorado's 4.3 million people (2000 Census data), 1 percent declare a Native American heritage. About 180 of those 43,000 Native peoples report a Golden address, which is probably the largest permanently settled Native American population that the city has experienced. Their traditions are alive and well, too.

The Legend of the Flat Pipe

The Arapaho explain their origins through the myth of the Flat Pipe. Before the Flat Pipe came into being, there were four worlds, or successive lives, of the earth. In the fourth world, the earth is covered with water, and the Pipe Person floats upon it, thinking and praying for the good. The Pipe Person received power and was able to call birds and animals to him to look for land beneath the waves. Two of these animals were red-headed duck and turtle. Red-headed duck tried to find land but failed. Turtle succeeded by bringing up mud on his feet. Pipe Person spread the mud on his pipe, dried it, and then blew the dirt to the four sacred directions. The earth was born. The Pipe Person then made the Sun, Moon, Man, Woman, Animals, Plants, and Seasons. These were the first Arapahos. Pipe Person told them how to live. They were given the Flat Pipe Bundle to care for and to use when communicating with Pipe Person.

The Bundle consisted of a stone pipe, a turtle, and an ear of corn wrapped in a deerskin. It was cared for by a priest who performed particular rituals throughout the year in return for help from Pipe Person. The priest's tipi was the first to be taken down when the band moved to a new location.

Gold seekers still search the soils of Clear Creek for color in the pan.

Chapter Three

The Gateway to Gold

For centuries, the area that would become the Front Range of Colorado was largely ignored by the rest of the world. It was a land that was traded back and forth between the Spanish, French, Americans, and Indians. Reports that filtered back to whatever government was overseeing the land at the time indicated the land was of little economic value: it was too dry to farm, there were no reports of vast mineral wealth, the high mountains were a natural barrier to transport and trade, and it was too far from any navigable waterway to prove useful as a way station to somewhere else.

Gold

This studio portrait ca. 1890 was taken in Golden, Colorado. The young miner or geologist sports a firearm at his waist and a rock hammer in his boot.

Gold. The small word has great meaning for cultures worldwide. It was the gleam of gold that drew the Spaniards through Mexico and into both North and South America. The Aztecs thought it was drippings from the sun itself. The Inca believed it was the solar essences fallen in fragments to the earth. Alchemists sought to turn base metals into gold through combinations of sorcery and chemistry. To ward off plagues, English citizens in the Middle Ages held slivers of gold coins in their mouths.

So, when gold was discovered on the American River in California in 1849, America sat up and took notice. Suddenly the American West held promise. The attraction proved overpowering for the thousands who traversed the Overland route or sailed around the Horn to reach El Dorado. Yet these thousands passed through the Rocky Mountains region on their way farther west without giving it so

Hoping for some "color," this participant in Golden Pioneer Museum's "Panning for the Past" tries his hand at panning for gold on the banks of Clear Creek.

much as a sidelong glance. It wasn't until a party of men from Georgia discovered gold along Cherry Creek—what is now present-day Denver—in 1858 that anyone really took notice of the Central Rocky Mountains. Even then, it wasn't until the middle of 1859 that the idea of the western Kansas Territory as a literal gold mine really took root.

William Green Russell, one of the Georgians, first heard about gold along the Front Range of the Rockies from some Cherokee Indians. The group had stopped to prospect there on their way to the California gold fields in 1849 and found some "color in the pan" along what would become known as Ralston Creek (present-day Arvada). Russell recalled this story, and in February 1858 again left Georgia, this time with two brothers and other Georgians, bound for Pikes Peak. The men prospected virtually every major creek north of the Arkansas River in their quest for gold.

Just as everyone was beginning to give up hope, they finally hit pay dirt along the Platte River above Cherry Creek. Reports of the find spread rapidly.

One of the first eastern newspapers to take note of the gold discoveries was the *Boston Evening Transcript*. On August 19, 1858, the paper extolled:

> Reports of gold on our western border have made quite a stir in our community, reawakening the auri sacra flames of our California adventurers, some of whom have gone in pursuit of the glittering treasure. (Quoted in Hafen, 1941)

Pocket scales and gold dust.

Just as rapidly as word spread, emigrants loaded up their belongings and hit the trails, bound for the gold fields. Rumors of the amount of gold being discovered grew with each retelling. Gold seemingly grew from the very earth. A man would scarcely have to turn a shovel of dirt before his fortune would surely be made. Thousands came west to experience the burgeoning gold rush.

One of the intrepid argonauts was Thomas L. Golden. Several of his letters to Eastern newspapers survive. In November 1858, he sent the following letter that was published in the *Missouri Republican* in January:

> I send you a specimen of our gold, which I dug myself. I have discovered new mines, twelve miles from Cherry creek, on a creek called Clear creek. The creek empties into South Platte, ten miles below where Cherry creek empties into the Platte.
>
> There are at this time fifty-three men at work on these mines, who average from $4 to $10 per day. Several old miners are at work in the mines. They say they are satisfied these mines are as good as any of the mines in California. We have prospected ten miles square. It will all pay wages by bringing water to it. We have organized a company of one hundred and begun a ditch, which we will complete by spring. It will afford plenty of water to work all the dry diggings. Yours, Thos. L. Golden. (Quoted in Hafen, 1941)

Christmas 1858 was a time for great celebration. Strikes were being reported virtually every week along the creeks from Pikes Peak to the Cache la Poudre River. A. O. McGrew relayed the good news to the *Omaha (Nebraska) Times* on December 29, 1858:

> The latest and richest gold diggings found are at the base of what is known as Table mountain, where already a town, known as Mountainvale, has been laid out and several houses erected while others are in progress of erection. (Quoted in Hafen, 1941)

This small settlement became Arapahoe Bar, then Arapahoe City, a town on the eastern outskirts of Golden City. It would not last beyond the playing out of the streams.

George A. Jackson, a friend of Thomas Golden, discovered gold near what is now Idaho Springs in January 1859.

Miners struggle up the steep trail on their way to Silver Plume and the Pelican Mine ca. 1870.

Gold Mining Tools

Pan—Shallow metal dish with outward flaring sides, sometimes with ridges to trap gold flakes.

Rocker—A wooden cradle with iron screen across the bottom; gravel is poured through first, then water, and the device is rocked back and forth.

Riffle—A wooden slat placed across a sluice bottom to catch gold. Many riffles are spaced down the length of the box and are sometimes coated with mercury.

Sluice—A square wooden box, open at the top with riffles to catch gold. Water and sediment are poured or routed through the box.

Long Tom—Similar to a rocker with the addition of a sluice.

After the Cherry Creek strike, the next major strikes that would ensure the future of the region came in 1859. Two men headed separately into the mountains west from Arapahoe City. Both followed Clear Creek. Unbeknownst to each other, they each made substantial strikes.

George Jackson, along with friend Thomas Golden and a man named Black Hawk, left Arapahoe City for the hills early in 1859. Jackson left Golden and Black Hawk behind and continued on alone. On January 7, at the junctions of North and South Clear Creeks, he hit pay dirt. Jackson knew he needed more equipment and supplies to work the digging. In addition, the weather, as it is wont to do in Colorado, had turned inclement, preventing any further action until better weather prevailed. Jackson did not want to risk losing his claim. He wrote in his journal: "Tom Golden is the only man who knows I found gold on the head of the creek, and as his mouth's as tight as a No. 4 beaver trap, I am not uneasy." Tom Golden wouldn't tell anyone.

John Gregory, a freighter from Gordon County, Georgia, made his strike just a few days after Jackson's. He had not intended to be prospecting in the area. Indeed, Gregory was on his way to the Frazier River in British Columbia, but was detained at Fort Laramie when he heard reports of gold. He panned his way down the South Platte River from northern Colorado, then up Clear Creek. The area he settled on working would become the boomtown of Central City. Gregory, also aware of the danger of public knowledge of his find, kept closed mouth as well. He returned to Georgia for the remainder of the winter, acquired sufficient supplies, and arrived back in the Territory in May. With $2,000 in hand courtesy of Golden City resident David K. Wall, Gregory was able to file his claim and begin work. Though Gregory made his strike in January, the officially recorded date of his strike is May 1859—when the strike was announced to the public and recorded. The Gregory lode, as it came to be known, has paid out over $85 million since its discovery. The gold rush had officially begun. Gregory, however, sold the diggings for $21,000. He left the Territory in September 1859 with $32,000 in gold dust in his possession.

Horace Greeley, newspaperman and promoter of the American West, confirmed these strikes but also admonished prospective argonauts that gold mining was expensive and extremely hard work. He also stressed that there were no direct routes to the gold fields, no navigable waterways, and that transport to reach the gold fields was rare and pricey. But his warnings fell on deaf ears. Thousands came, many with little more than a gold pan and the clothes on their back.

Within about a year, the streams of the Colorado Territory played out. Little gold could be had by panning or from the sluice box. It seemed the new El Dorado was a bust, or so thought many of the men who had come to the region expecting a repeat of the California gold fields. The fundamental difference between the gold of California and that of Colorado is how it washes out from the rock formations. In California, the majority of the gold that spawned the 1849 gold rush was lode gold, which washes out primarily in large nuggets and flakes. Colorado's gold, called float gold, washed out in small flecks with an occasional nugget or flake. While placer mining could continue indefinitely in California, speculative or hard rock mining began early in Colorado. Between 1858 and 1962, 16,558 ounces of gold were removed from the gravels of Jefferson County, Colorado, worth more than $6.9 million, most of it from Clear Creek (calculated at the 2004 price of $418 an ounce).

Still seeking riches, many travel to Black Hawk and Central City to try their luck at the casinos that now line the streets of both mountain towns.

Golden's role in gold mining would have seemingly ended with the demise of placer mining, but in fact, with the success of hard rock mining, her role grew. The town was fortuitously, albeit intentionally, situated at the mouth of Clear Creek Canyon. Mercantiles and mining supply stores were among the first businesses to spring up in town. Miners heading toward Jackson's diggings at Chicago Creek or Gregory's Lode in Leavenworth Gulch would have little choice but to pass through Golden. Supplies could be had in the mountains, but they would be more costly than in the valley. Golden was also on the return route for the miners who had not made their fortunes in the gravels of Central City. They could take the opportunity to sell their equipment back to the Boston Company store before catching a stagecoach or wagon train back east.

Although none of these young explorers made their fortune in the Panning for the Past field school, July 2003, some do still find gold and garnets.

Golden provided another valuable service to the mining industry—smelting, which is integral to the gold mining process. Utilizing her abundant coal and fire clay resources, the town gained prominence by operating large-scale smelters and nearly dominating the ore reduction market in northern Colorado.

Golden Smelter employees include foreman Culberson, Maurice Hoyt, Burt Daly, and Mike McIntyre.

Glossary of Mining Terms

Crofutt's Grip-Sack Guide to Colorado contained a very thorough list of commonly used mining terms from the American, Mexican, Spanish, and Cornish miners.

Arrastra—A mill for grinding ores. A crude contrivance, circular in form, where ores are ground to powder by attrition of heavy stones secured by ropes to a long pole—about midway—one end of which is fastened on a pivot in the center of the circle and the other end hauled around by hand or animal power.

Assaying—Finding the percentage of a given metal in ore or bullion.

Blower—A smelting furnace.

Bonanza—Is good luck; a large body of ore, a rich strike; an abundant treasure.

Chimney—A chimney-shaped body of ore, generally perpendicular.

Cord of Ore—128 cubic feet of broken ore; about seven tons in quartz rock.

Core—Miners usually work but six hours at a time. The "forenoon core" is from 6:00 a.m. to noon; the "afternoon core" from noon to 6:00 p.m.; "night core" from 6:00 p.m. to midnight; "last core" from midnight to 6:00 a.m.; four shifts.

Diggings—Name applied to placers being worked.

Drift—The excavation made for a road underground.

End Lines—The lines bounding the ends of a claim.

Fissure Vein—A fissure or crack in the earth's crust filled with mineral matter. The two walls are always of the same geological formation.

Float—Loose rock or isolated masses of ore, or ore detached from the original formation.

Flookan—A cross-vein composed of clay.

Free Gold—Gold easily separated from the quartz or dirt.

Little Giant—A moveable nozzle attached to hydraulic pipes.

Lode—Any zone or belt of mineralized rock lying with the boundaries clearly separating it from the neighboring rock.

Mill-Run—A test of quality of ore after reduction.

Outfit—Tools, etc., needed in the business; provisions, etc.

Outcrop—That portion of a vein appearing on the surface.

Pay Streak—That seam in crevice containing the mineral.

Smelting—Reducing the ore in furnaces to metals.

Stamps—Machines for crushing ores.

Tailings—The auriferous earth that has once been washed and deprived of the greater portion of the gold it contained.

Vein—Aggregations of mineral matter in fissures of rocks.

Golden Smelter ca. 1888. The smelting process kept Golden's skies filled with smoke. Today it is rare for Golden to have gloomy skies.

One method of gold recovery from ore is through the smelting process. Stamp mills crush the gold to a powder-fine consistency. The auriferous powder is hydrated and passed over mercury-coated copper plates, where it is coated on one side with mercury. The resulting gold-mercury amalgam is then heated to the boiling point of mercury and turned into "gold sponge." After the mercury is vaporized off, the sponge is heated in crucibles to create bullion. The resulting bullion can then be melted into bars or coinage.

By the early 1870s, Golden Smelting Works had opened. Many of the needed resources could be found within just a few miles of the city center. There was fire clay for the manufacture of fire brick, coal for the fires, and lime and mercury in the area, plus the construction of railroads was imminent. While the early ore received at the smelting works was considered to be of poor quality with a low ratio of gold to other minerals, that changed quickly, and the operation was soon turning out tens of thousands of dollars in bullion each week. By 1873, the plant was smelting copper and silver as well.

By 1879, Thomas Corbett had compiled the Colorado Directory of Mines. He noted that in Jefferson County there were the French Smelting Works, Trenton Dressing and Smelting, Valley Smelting Works, and the Golden Smelting Company. All were located in western and northern Golden. Operating at peak production, the plants could process from fifteen to sixty tons of ore daily per smelter. By the turn of the century, the smelters had closed. In 1901, Franklin Carpenter built a smelter in town for highly pyretiferrous ores (high iron content), but it closed permanently in 1911.

Mercury was used in hydraulic mining as well as smelting. Hydraulic mining, developed during the California gold rush, involves diverting a watercourse to produce a significant blast of water strong enough to break up large pieces of rock. The resulting sediment travels through a sluice or riffle box used to recover the free gold. Mercury would be used to coat the riffles to "catch" the gold, thereby forming an amalgam. About 10 percent to 30 percent of the mercury used in

Little White Ash miners ca. 1880. Children as young as five years old were often employed in mines, performing such tasks as carrying tools and "necessary buckets" in and out of the mines. By the age of fourteen, a young man was eligible to work as a miner.

this process was lost downstream. Upstream from Golden, this process was used to recover gold in various gulches and tributaries of Clear Creek.

For decades, fish were nearly nonexistent in Clear Creek. Only through diligent cleanup and management has the stream again become clean, and fish have begun populating it. Placer mining still occurs to a limited extent. Throughout the year, several intrepid sorts can be found knee-deep in Clear Creek wielding shovel and shaker with moderate success.

Coal

Coal, though abundant in the Golden area, is in small deposits and is extremely expensive to mine on a large scale. In most places, coal beds run horizontally below the surface along the foothills. Many are vertical, including all the beds in the Golden area. The quality of the coal varies from lignite to anthracite. Most of Golden's coal is subbituminous.

Coal outcrops on Dry (Van Bibber) Creek were discovered in 1860, and Edward Berthoud noted other outcrops near Golden early in the 1860s. He indicated the coal was of an excellent quality, free of sulphur and only 3 percent to 4 percent ash, so it would burn very hot. By 1867, small-scale mining operations had opened on Green Mountain, six miles south of Golden. Four mines were in operation in 1875, supplying Central City, Black Hawk, Denver, Morrison, and Golden with more than 218,000 tons.

The White Ash Mine opened in 1877. It was a large, well-funded operation on the south side of Clear Creek. The *Colorado Transcript* notes that it had a 200 horsepower hoist and could lift forty tons of coal per day. But apparently a rift arose between the mines and the Colorado Central Railroad.

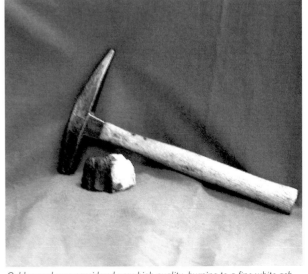

Golden coal was considered very high quality, burning to a fine white ash.

Train cars were to be supplied to the mines to transport the coal, but the Colorado Central had a number of mines to which it would not deliver more than a single car. As a result, the mines were unable to move their coal, causing layoffs and other problems. The *Transcript* caught wind of the issue and promptly issued a firm rebuke to the Colorado Central, admonishing the guilty parties with "talk about trying to build up Golden." The problem was quickly resolved, and production resumed.

Strikes were a common problem in Colorado mines. The working conditions were dangerous, the hours long, and the pay low. Workers struck at the White Ash in 1892 and 1895. But the strikes at Golden were never profitable because the mines were never profitable. The beds lie vertically, so it cost 20 percent more to mine here than anywhere else, thereby making the coal more expensive than elsewhere and reducing mine profits.

Coal mining, like any mining endeavor, was rife with danger. Accidents were almost guaranteed to happen. However, Golden was rather fortunate in that the mines within her vicinity experienced fewer accidents than most mining regions witness. Given that the coal seams were nearly vertical, that is an amazing feat. Colorado enacted mine safety laws in 1883, but the U.S. Bureau of Mines did not come into existence until 1910 to oversee such laws.

Most of the mine accidents reported in the *Colorado Transcript* and *Golden Globe* dealt with mechanical problems. For example, in January 1884, a piston rod broke at the White Ash Mine and dropped an ore cart down the mineshaft. Fortunately, no one was injured when the cart fell. Miners were occasionally buried by rock falls, as was the case in September 1884 when two men were buried in separate accidents in the same mine. One died from his injuries; the other escaped with minor injuries.

By far, the worst mining accident in Golden's history occurred at the White Ash Mine on September 9, 1889. Three years earlier, a fire had broken out at the 280-foot level inside the

Coal mine head frame, White Ash Mine, Golden, Colorado, ca. 1895.

Miners' lives were hard and often short, with a life span of about twenty-two years. Men often lost their hearing due to working in proximity to loud tools and machinery. Ca. 1890.

White Ash. The smoke grew so bad that the miners had to leave the mine until it cleared out. The shaft was walled up, and it was hoped the fire would burn itself out. But it did not extinguish and continued to burn, gradually disintegrating a ninety-foot wall between the White Ash and the Loveland Mines, located on the north side of Clear Creek. The Loveland Mine had been closed for nearly a decade, one of its shafts flooded with water from Clear Creek.

On the afternoon of September 9, ten men were working at the 730-foot depth in the White Ash when water suddenly began rushing into the mine. Unaware of the unfolding disaster, the surface hoist operator tried to lower the miner's cage to the bottom of the shaft, but he couldn't get the cage to go beyond the 400-foot level and was receiving no signals from the operator at the bottom. A man climbed down the shaft some distance and heard the roar of water pouring into the mine. They then knew the ten men were lost. A mine investigator determined that the White Ash fire had penetrated into the Loveland Mine's flooded tunnel, allowing the water to pour unchecked into the White Ash. It was estimated that a recovery effort would take upwards of three months. A stone monument marks the location of the shaft where the men met their deaths. The mine closed in 1895. In 1900, the Golden Commercial Club, a predecessor of the Chamber of Commerce, proposed reopening the White Ash Mine. It estimated it would cost $20,000 to open the shaft and pump out the water. The Loveland shaft on the north side would also be reopened. However, nothing ever came of this proposal.

Other dangers lurked for miners as well, as the early tools of the trade produced a tremendous amount of dust. Dust was a silent killer for both gold and coal miners. Silicosis killed many early gold miners, and black lung stalked the coal miner. The most infamous of these tools was invented in the 1870s by C. H. Shaw of Denver. It was a type of hammer drill nicknamed "the widow maker." The tool was used to drill holes in the rock for placement of explosives such as black blasting powder. The drill cuttings were sucked into the lungs of the unwitting miner running the drill. As a result, the average expected life span of a miner working with a widow maker was three to five years. It wasn't until 1897 that a hammer drill using water to wet down the tailings was invented.

Coal is no longer mined in the Golden area but still is elsewhere in Colorado. The Leyden mine, located north of Golden, was the last local coal mine to close. The U.S. Geological Survey estimates that between 1867 and 1956, 10 million tons of coal was extracted from beneath Jefferson County, most of it from Morrison northward to the Boulder County line. It estimates that another 250 million tons still lies beneath the surface. The remnants of the mines, including head frames, tipples, loading docks, and slag piles, can be found in the countryside near Golden.

Clay

It is often incorrectly assumed that Golden took its name from the vast wealth of gold that lay practically at its doorstep. In fact, Golden was most probably christened for a man named Thomas Golden. Golden has remarkably little gold in its streams and earth. What it has in abundance is clay. Rufus Sage noted the clay outcrops in the journals of his 1843 trip up Vasquez Forks, now

Parfet (par-fet) clay mine ca. 1940. This worker is using a hand auger to drill a placement for dynamite.

Train cars carried clay to tipples on the Denver, Lakewood, and Golden rail line, ca. 1940.

known as Clear Creek. Clay is the bane of the Colorado gardener's existence. The entire Front Range has copious amounts of it. Colorado has it all—from moisture-retaining clays that cause unstable soils, to extremely high-grade, low-moisture, and low-iron clays that are exceptional for earthenware and terra cotta. In 1915, G. Montague Butler sampled and studied most of the clays along the Front Range and made recommendations for their uses.

Between the vertical layers of sandstone that border Golden to the west are extensive deposits of several varieties of both high-grade and medium-grade clays. In 1877, George Washington Parfet, weary of the family trade in coal mining, hit upon the idea of mining clay. Cities throughout the region were growing, and brick was rapidly becoming the preferred building material. It is fire-resistant and infinitely more durable than wood. With investment partners H. M. Rubey and William S. Woods, Parfet began mining the clay of the Laramie Formation west of Golden.

In the days before mechanization, clay mining was similar to hard rock mining but without many of the side effects. For clay mines in the east, a strip mining procedure was employed because the beds lie hor-

Though the Golden Fire and Pressed Brick Company no longer exists, one can still find Golden-manufactured bricks around town.

izontal to the surface of the overlying ground. Along the upturned hog-backs of the Colorado Front Range, a different approach has to be used. The clay in and around Golden crops out at the surface, making it easy to locate a seam. First, an adit is driven into the seam. This is a type of tunnel without an opening at the other end that is driven into a hillside to access a mineral deposit. Drifts, or tunnels, leading up and away are dug from the adit up into the seam; charges are set, then detonated. The resultant collapses are called glory holes, which are then mucked into carts and taken away. In the days when Parfet first began mining clay, all work was done by hand. Men used hand-held augers to drill the holes for the dynamite charges; workers with shovels loaded the clay into carts, then rolled the carts down to the tipple, where the clay was transferred into a train car.

Golden and Denver both had fire brick companies during the late 1800s and into the early 1900s. The Parfet's clay contained 10 percent kaolin-ite; it also had a wide range of vitrification. These factors made it excep-tional for the production of fire brick. One of the Parfet's biggest cus-tomers for one hundred years was the Denver Brick and Pipe Company. Train cars from the Denver Intermountain Railway were loaded with tons of clay, which was transported into the brick plant. The clay was formed and baked into yellowish-tan bricks that were used throughout the area. Denver Brick was the largest manufacturer of brick in the region until the 1930s. The Parfet mines also sold clay to the Gjeisbeck Pottery Company, the Herold Pottery Company, and the Coors Porcelain Plant. At the early part of the twentieth century, the mines were taking out fifty to sixty train carloads of clay per week, or about 1,600 tons.

Parfet family ca. 1895 (from left): Mattie, Edward, Grant, Caleb, George, Jr., Ray, and George, Sr. The family was descended from Welsh coal miners.

George W. Parfet family ca. 1900.

In 1901, a coal seam was struck in the mine. It was worked for several years before being abandoned. George Parfet had originally intended to drift toward the White Ash Mine.

In 1910, the Parfet land was preserved through a series of partnerships and purchases so that it could continue to be mined without fear of development overtaking the land. George W. Parfet died in 1924. His sons, George Jr. and Grant, took over the business. In 1940, George Jr. died, and the business passed to his son, William George Parfet. The years of World War II turned out to be very good for the brick industry. Though growth slowed nationwide, the Denver Federal Center was taking shape. Its major tenant became the Remington Arms Plant, a brick structure that made ammunition. It needed a great deal of clay to construct the plant, and Parfet clay came to the rescue.

By the 1920s, the State School of Mines was doing what it could to assist in the development of the clay resources in Colorado, including Golden's mines. The school added ceramic engineering classes to train men for employment in an escalating industry.

After World War II, the Parfet clay operation became mechanized, and a Bay City shovel was purchased. Prior to the purchase of the shovel, the seams were excavated only to a depth of about sixty feet between the sandstone "fins," or ridges, on either side of the seam. It was simply too dangerous for a man with a hand shovel to be any deeper than that. The Bay City shovel enabled the seam to be excavated to depths of more than one hundred feet. The shovel could scoop up hundreds of pounds of clay at a time, deposit it in a cart, then swing back into the seam for the next load. Carts were still pushed by hand to the railroad tipple for transport to Denver. By the 1950s, railroad transport was replaced with trucks, and additional heavy equipment was added. The mine purchased an American Dragline and American Shovel. These enabled more clay to be mined even faster. By the 1960s, Colorado was the leading producer of refractory clays in the Rocky Mountain region.

In the 1970s, William retired, and his son, William "Chip" Parfet, Jr., took over the operation. At the time, mining regulations were becoming more stringent with very specialized concerns related to employee safety and environmental impacts, necessitating major changes within the operation. Even more mechanization took place with the additions of front end loaders and diesel trucks. Denver Brick ceased to be a customer of the Parfet mine. Lakewood Brick became its primary customer. Because of improved methods and more mechanization, in one year's time, from 2001 to 2002, the clay mine moved more clay than it had in the entire preceding 124 years.

Golden has virtually encompassed the land that was once clay mines. Housing developments and office parks sit adjacent to the old pits and remaining fins of Dakota Sandstone. Land adjacent to the Parfet's primary mine, the Rockwell, was acquired by the City of Golden for a golf course. The city needed additional land to make the course a reality, so in June 2001 it purchased the Rockwell Mine. It has now been reclaimed for the course. The mine to the south of the Rockwell, the Rubey, will become open space with a bike path and interpretive trails.

Reclaiming a clay mine is fundamentally different from reclaiming a gold mine. In clay mining, the clay and some surrounding sandstone or siltstone are removed. There are no hazardous minerals disturbed or toxic chemicals used in the process. Thus, reclamation, while expensive, is markedly easier. The Parfet Mine #1, located to the south of Golden, was

In 2003, the City of Golden opened the Fossil Trace Golf Course on land reclaimed from the Parfet clay mine. The golf course now provides some of the most beautiful vistas in the Golden area.

reclaimed in 1988. At the time, the C-470 highway was under construction; 600,000 cubic yards of fill material (soil) from the construction was used to cap the mine. It was then seeded to promote native plant growth. The Rockwell was reclaimed by the City of Golden as a golf course, Fossil Trace. It would have taken $1 million to reclaim it in a similar fashion to the Parfet Mine #1. Reclamation of the Rubey began in 2001 and was completed at the end of 2003. That marked the end of clay mining in Golden. The mines will all have been reclaimed, and a 125-year piece of history will be filed away.

Other materials have been mined and quarried in Golden as well, among them uranium, copper, crushed rock, limestone, mica, and gravel. In 1954, a substantial uranium strike was made northwest of Golden. The Swartzwalder Mine, from that strike, became one of the most profitable uranium mines in the state. Uranium was also found associated with coal mines, including those at Leyden and Morrison. Copper strikes were inevitable, as much of Colorado's gold is found with copper. Henry Koch had a productive copper strike at Chimney Gulch. Copper was one of the metals recovered by the smelters. Crushed rock and aggregate have been actively

quarried for more than a century. Much of it was and is used as riprap for road building and concrete aggregate. In 1900, Denver was mining on South Table Mountain to acquire rock to macadamize the streets. North Table Mountain was quarried for the volcanic rock. Limestone outcrops to the west were quarried for mortar and smelter flux, but operations ceased with the demise of the smelting industry. Sand and gravel are still removed from the area. About 10 million cubic yards have been removed since quarrying began, much of it coming from Clear Creek. Oil seeps have been found throughout Jefferson County, but no successful wells have ever been tapped.

Metal mining has all but ceased in the Golden area. Mineral extraction is too costly in an area where the beds lie at odd angles or there are insufficient veins to make it profitable. In addition, as was noted nearly fifty years ago, development continues to encroach on former mining or quarrying areas. Essentially, Golden's history as a frontier mining town is over.

View of Golden looking east.

Golden ca. 1863. Visible is the Loveland Building, the Golden Mill (still under construction). The Boston Company building is just behind and to the right of the mill and barely visible.

Chapter Four

**Foundations of a Community and
Foundations of a State**

Groups traveling west often used guides such as this one to prepare for their trips. Some authors had often never been west of the Mississippi River.

They came from all corners of the United States and its territories, seeking the new California, the next get-rich-quick opportunity. Drawn by fantastic descriptions of monstrous nuggets of gold lying close at hand, they dismissed negative critiques such as the "Great American Desert" in light of the possibilities for immense wealth that surely abounded in the western Kansas Territory.

Within the span of one year's time, more than 100,000 people "jumped off" from places like St. Joseph, Missouri, and Kansas City bound for the Pikes Peak gold fields. Only about half the enterprising adventurers arrived safely in the Territory. Famine, lack of grazing fodder, unpre-

Joel and Matilda Palmer arrived in Golden on May 8, 1860, and settled on the banks of Clear Creek, east of North Table Mountain. Their third child, Charles, was born in October 1860.

dictable weather, hostile Indians, raiders, and a variety of other hazards awaited the unsuspecting emigrants along the route. Others succumbed to cholera, "mountain fever," and a host of other maladies exacerbated by the harsh traveling conditions. Graves littered the prairie from one end of a trail to the other. Matilda Palmer, an early Golden City pioneer, recalled that their party would build a cooking fire over the grave of the recently deceased so that the Indians wouldn't realize it was a grave and dig it up. In actuality, most Plains tribes had an aversion to the recently deceased and any possible malingering bad spirit. It is likely that the Palmer group, like most

Artist Michael Harden used several historic photographs as inspiration to create his vision of early Golden.

Tent settlements often marked the locations where towns would soon grow in the Colorado Territory.

travelers, were ill-informed by a manual or article written by someone who had never traveled to the West.

Bad advice plagued many of the westward-bound. Guide books and newspaper articles carried glorious descriptions of the region and contained helpful advice on reaching the gold fields in good order. Once the travelers arrived in the western Kansas Territory, the amenities were not all that had been promised. The "great cities rivaling those of the East" were little more than tent cities or hastily constructed wooden structures huddled around muddy streets. Prices were exorbitant, and after having spent every dime for the trip west, many families couldn't afford even the most basic rations. And then there were the gold fields. By mid-1860, most of the placer mining had ceased, and speculative mining had begun in earnest. This differed vastly from California, where much of the mining was done with a pan and sluice box. Pick, shovel, and dynamite were more than some people had bargained on.

The "go-backers," as they were called, returned east with a great deal less than they had arrived with. Gone were the wagons full of clothing, furniture, and knickknacks; gone were the teams of oxen and milk cows. They were fortunate to return home with the clothing on their backs and enough money to buy passage on a stage or supply train. D. C. Oakes, who had written glowing accounts of his first trip to the gold fields, often found his name in the discussions of the go-backers or even on their wagons. One epithet of the time read: "Here lie the remains of D. C. Oakes: Who was the starter of this damned hoax." William Byers, editor of the *Rocky Mountain News* and ardent supporter of the emigration, also featured prominently in a go-backer poem. Newspapers in the early 1860s printed the names of those who had "seen the elephant," decided it wasn't worth it, and had gone home.

Those who remained began to do what people in the wilderness always do—organize. Many were interested only in pursuing the elusive sparkle in the rivers and streams, while others realized the true wealth would come not from the bottom of a gold pan but from the pockets of the men and women holding the pans. On May 6, 1859, John H. Gregory, an itinerant miner from Gordon County, Georgia, made the strike that would launch the "Pikes Peak or Bust" gold rush. Word of the strike, courtesy of Horace Greeley, made its way rapidly eastward, and the people came. Towns sprang up across the Plains—Denver City, Auraria City, Arapahoe Bar, Golden Gate, Spanish Bar, Idaho, Black Hawk. Of every size and demeanor, they seemed to materialize virtually overnight from the clay soils of the western Kansas Territory. One among many beat the odds and survived and thrived—Golden City.

Boston Company ad from the Western Mountaineer, *December 23, 1859.*

As the emigration came pouring in from the several routes across the Plains, all were pushing for the mountains, and here nearly all halted to store a portion of their provisions and send out their prospecting parties. It became evident at once that this was a good point to build up a town.

George West
Western Mountaineer
December 7, 1859

Arrival of the Boston Company

George West was nothing if not optimistic about the prospects of the budding town on the banks of Clear Creek or Vasquez Fork, as it was often called. When word reached Massachusetts of gold discoveries in the western Kansas Territory, West and several friends each pitched in $150 to found the Mechanics Mining and Trade Company. They filled fourteen wagons with supplies and headed west. West, a printer by trade, encountered William Byers when the company arrived in Auraria City. Byers was looking for someone who could run a printing press to issue a special edition of the *Rocky Mountain News* and confirm John Gregory's gold strike. West and his companions, Mark Blunt and William Summers, printed the special edition of the *Rocky Mountain News* for Byers. The men soon moved on to a settlement on the banks of Clear Creek.

Upon arrival, the men found little more than a collection of tents surrounding David Wall's farm. Several homestead claims were filed, but no permanent structures had yet been built. The potential was evident: everyone on their way to Gregory's or Jackson's Diggings would have to pass through this valley. Clear Creek afforded the most convenient avenue to both areas. This was where the newly reorganized Boston Company would put down roots.

Boston Company store ca.1859. The Boston Company building was constructed under the direction of George West and is considered to be the first permanent building in Golden. The supply store housed Golden's first newspaper, the Western Mountaineer, and the first post office. Courtesy Stephen H. Hart Library, Colorado Historical Society.

This monument in Parfet Park marks the site of the Boston Company store. The marker was placed there by the Mount Lookout Chapter of the Daughters of the American Revolution in 1927.

On June 16, 1859, the first organizational meeting of the Golden City Town Company was held. In attendance was nearly the entire human population of the valley, including David Wall and his family, the Boston Company, the Boyd family, and a handful of others. The town boasted a toll bridge at T. P. Boyd's property, a few farms, some placer claims, and little else. By July, there was a steam-powered sawmill. Not to be outdone, Captain George West and his Boston Company erected the first permanent structure in the town, a combination mercantile and print shop. West launched publication of the *Western Mountaineer* newspaper in December.

By late December, John McIntyre had incorporated the St. Vrain, Golden City, and Colorado Wagon Road—a major passage to the mining camps of South Park. Several hotels had opened as well, affording travelers the opportunity and luxury of remaining in the blossoming town and partaking of all it had to offer. West noted in the December 14, 1859, edition of the *Western Mountaineer* that a number of beautiful ladies were already gracing Golden City.

Golden City grew quickly with the right combination of people to ensure her success as a town. Freight lines, mail service, and a myriad of other services sprang up within months of the town's founding. William Austin Hamilton Loveland, a Mexican-American War veteran from Chatham, Massachusetts, arrived in Golden in June 1859. He immediately set to work constructing a two-story mercantile on Golden City's main thoroughfare. A legend abounds that West and Loveland had a little wager on who would complete the first permanent building in town. The story goes that both buildings were ready for shingling, but Loveland did not have any shingles. Spying a pile of shingles outside the Boston Company in the dark of night, Loveland liberated the shingles from West. He later returned the shingles, giving West the honor of finishing first.

George West arrived in Golden in June 1859. In 1861, he made three round trips between Golden and St Joseph, Missouri, bringing much-needed supplies for the burgeoning town. During the Civil War, he served as a captain in the Second Colorado Volunteers from May 1862 until the end of the war in 1865. He became the adjutant general of the Colorado National Guard in 1887.

This depiction of the interior of the Loveland building shows W. A. H. Loveland, George West, and E. L. Berthoud serving in the territorial government. Michael Moylan, 1999.

A Golden Opportunity?

A longstanding debate concerns why Golden was chosen as the name for the town. Reasonably successful placer (gold panning) efforts were undertaken to the east of the valley at Arapahoe Bar during 1858 and 1859, but not enough gold was recovered to justify naming an entire town for it. To the west of the area was a yellowish rock formation that some thought looked like a gate, thereby giving rise to the town of Golden Gate. Some wrote that the name was related to the town site, representing a golden business opportunity. These accounts were written long after the founding of the town. Memories fade, and history begins to take on the hue of the rose-colored glasses through which the present often views events long ago.

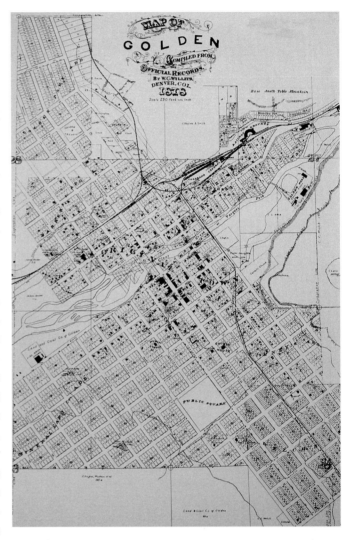

The most likely explanation for the town's name lies in an obscure set of letters and documents dating from the precise time of the gold rush. Thomas Golden came to the territory with a party of men who settled in Auraria on Cherry Creek for a while, buying lots and dipping their pans in the water before moving on toward the foothills. Land records indicate that Tom Golden was extremely prominent in Arapahoe Bar and Golden Gate City, even holding public office at Arapahoe Bar. He eventually sold his land interests in the valley and moved into the mountains before being lost to history. It is conceivable that men such as David Wall and John Pounder, early valley residents, knew Thomas Golden and thought highly enough of the man to name a town for him.

Territorial Government

Within a few months, the conglomeration of towns along the Front Range and into the mountains was clamoring for an independent status. As it was no longer politically or economically advantageous to be part of Kansas Territory, the Territory of Jefferson came into being. It was generally described by the southwestern boundary of the Louisiana Purchase, part of the Mexican secession, and portions of the northernmost Texas secession—basically the square dimension of Colorado today. A provisional government was formed, and application was made to the U.S. Congress for recognition. Provisional Governor R. W. Steele was told that no additional states or territories would be named after presidents, so a new name would have to be selected. Many names were chosen and discarded, from Idaho to Dakota. Eventually the founders went back to the Spanish exploration of the region and settled on Colorado, meaning "red." The provisional government was not wholly accepted by the residents of the Territory. It is said, "Golden was the only settlement that wholly submitted to the provisional government."

Organizers of the Territory went back to the drawing board. Towns throughout the area held elections, counties were formed, and laws enacted. So, on February 26, 1861, Congress willingly recognized the new Territory, and William Gilpin was appointed governor. But Gilpin did not start out on a good foot with many residents. He knew that many Southern sympathizers resided in the Territory, so to avert trouble during the imminent War between the States, he instituted loyalty codes and oaths of allegiance to the Union. Gilpin was soon replaced by John Evans.

Problems continued to arise when the territorial capital was established at Camp Creek (now Old Colorado City), in the shadow of Pikes Peak. The town was little more than a cluster of cabins, forcing the legislators to camp out and do their own cooking and laundry. A near riot ensued, and the capital was transferred to Denver. Among the laws enacted in 1862 were those to organize a militia and establish judicial districts. The act designating Camp Creek (Colorado City) as the capital was repealed, and a new act established Golden City as the new territorial capital. Subsequent assemblies were convened in Golden City, then moved to Denver until 1867, when the capital was permanently transferred to Denver.

The first Jefferson County Courthouse was built in 1877 at the top of Washington Avenue. The building was torn down in July 1963.

Reminiscent of the original structure, this condominium complex is built on the site of the original courthouse.

The Jefferson County Courthouse complex, built in 1993, is the third such building to serve the county.

Elections and County Government

Mayor Chuck Baroch, 2003. Courtesy City of Golden.

Jefferson County's first elections were held on January 2, 1860. Votes were cast not only for county leadership but also for a county seat. Of the 711 votes cast, Golden City received 401, Arapahoe City 288, and Bergen 22. Golden City became and remains the seat of Jefferson County. For the leadership positions, Walter Pollard was elected sheriff, William McKay and T. P. Boyd became associate judges, and Eli Carter county recorder. In February, postmasters for the western portion of the Kansas Territory were assigned. Samuel Brown became Jefferson County's first postmaster. For years, argument raged about how the postal system was gouging the western territories for postage. At the time, there was not a universal flat rate for the United States and her territories. Westerners paid far more per pound than did easterners: fifty cents per letter and ten cents per newspaper.

When Golden City held its first municipal elections on April 10, 1860, J. W. Stanton was elected mayor, S. M. Breath town recorder, W. C. Simpson town marshal, and William Loveland town treasurer. Eight trustees rounded out the city government. The trustee system was changed in 1879 to a city council structure.

Bayard Taylor visited Golden City in 1866. His observations on the Territory served as encouragement to many in the East wondering if the enterprise would survive. In a letter from Central City dated June 23, 1866, Taylor writes of Golden City:

Golden City enjoys the distinction of being the capital of Colorado Territory...The population is not more than three or four hundred, and the place has a quiet and rather forlorn appearance at present. It possesses, nevertheless, several substantial stores, a school-house, two flour-mills and a manufactory of fire-brick. From this time forward, it will rise in importance.

This ballot box was used in many of Golden's early elections.

Golden Street Name Changes

Pre-1904 Name	Post-1904 Name		
Junction Street	First Street	Fourth Street	Fourteenth Street
Golden Street	Fourth Street	Seventh Street	Seventeenth Street
King Street	Seventh Street	Tenth Street	Twentieth Street
Platte Street	Tenth Street	Thirteenth Street	Twenty-third Street
Third Street	Thirteenth Street	Nettie Street	Elm Street
Sixth Street	Sixteenth Street	Park Street	Third Street
Ninth Street	Nineteenth Street	Payette Street	Sixth Street
Twelfth Street	Twenty-second Street	Garrison Street	Ninth Street
Helen Street	Maple Street	Second Street	Twelfth Street
Main Street	Second Street	Fifth Street	Fifteenth Street
Gregory Street	Fifth Street	Eighth Street	Eighteenth Street
Wall Street	Eighth Street	Eleventh Street	Twenty-first Street
First Street	Eleventh Street	Fourteenth Street	Twenty-fourth Street
		Esther Street	Birch Street

In 1871, Golden was formally incorporated. The town was divided into four wards with two overlying districts, primarily to provide for the collection of the poll tax—$2.50 or two days labor. In 1945, the last popularly elected mayor of Golden was chosen—Joseph Kellogg. As early as 1923, the residents had been discussing the need for a city manager rather than a mayor. Little was done beyond discussion and editorializing in the newspapers until October 11, 1947, when a special election was held, altering the city charter to provide for the hiring of a city manager.

Looking south on Washington Avenue ca. 2003.

On February 12, 1948, it was announced that Henry Rolfes, a twenty-seven-year-old city manager from Sylvan Lake, Michigan, would take up the reins of city government on March 15. The starting salary was a hefty $4,250 per year. The city would still have a mayor, but the City Council would choose him or her from among its ranks. The city manager would handle all of the day-to-day duties of running the growing city.

Golden voters changed their minds once again in 2002 when they decided to return to having a popularly elected mayor. The city manager would still handle the day-to-day city operations. Charles "Chuck" Baroch became the last mayor chosen by the City Council. The 2003 elections marked the first mayoral vote of the people in Golden since the Joe Kellogg vs. H. W. Ryland race in 1945. Today, the City Council is composed of seven members—four are elected from wards, two are elected from the districts, and one is elected as mayor.

In 1868, Golden City was laid out into blocks and lots. Many of the names honored the female relatives of the town's founders. The first of two street name changes occurred in 1881. Several streets on the north side of Clear Creek were standardized to match street names on the south side. The second and more major change came in 1904 when the numeric streets were essentially flip-flopped and many others incorporated into the numbering system or renamed outright.

Looking south on Washington Avenue, the Jefferson County Courthouse is visible in the distance ca. 1880.

Golden Police Department, 1945. From left: Wes Travis, Everet Hall, Charlie White, Dave Helps, and Floyd Bishops.

Golden did not have a jail until the courthouse was constructed in 1877. Prisoners were often housed in local boardinghouses and hotels.

K-9 Handler Officer Bob Wilson and K-9 Officer Ivo, a Dutch shepherd.

Law Enforcement

As evidenced by the election of a sheriff in the first county elections, law enforcement was considered to be a vital need. Golden elected a town marshal in 1860, and a night watchman was appointed in the subsequent years. The early Golden Police Department was under the jurisdiction of the Jefferson County Sheriff's Department. The Police Department's role was fairly small; maintaining order, issuing tickets for violations, and rounding up stray animals was often the extent of its duties. C. P. Hoyt was elected to the town marshal position in 1871. Carlos Lake became the first recognized town police chief in 1878.

The duties and the crimes encountered by the Golden marshals changed dramatically over the decades. In May 1901, the *Transcript* noted: "A gang of tinhorn gamblers...common toughs male and female...from the slums of Denver, took possession of a goodly portion of the eastern part of Golden last Sunday." They apparently had brought with them several kegs of Zang's beer to liven up the party. The police were roundly chastised for not encouraging the ruffians to vacate the area. By and large, much of the turn-of-the-century crime consisted of theft.

Prohibition was in effect nationwide throughout the 1920s. Golden and its surrounding areas had a booming moonshine business. City and county police reports of the period record a still bust nearly every week. Forest fires, always a problem in Colorado, occurred more frequently during Prohibition. Many were caused by fires from stills that were hidden in the hills. During the 1930s, most of the crimes were burglaries and larcenies, with an occasional murder. A large headline announced a high-speed chase in March 1938 when a patrolman spotted a stolen car and chased the perpetrator down Washington Avenue. The man escaped.

Crime has changed with the times, as has law enforcement. Golden's Police Department has grown from a town marshal and night watchman to a police chief, hired in 1921, to a present-day force of forty uniformed officers plus administrative personnel, reserve officers, a crime lab technician, and numerous support personnel. The ability to track speeders with radar came to Golden in 1960. Since the early 1990s, the Golden Police Department has had a K-9 unit as well.

Four hard-working dogs sniff out drugs, explosives, and criminals. The department's mission is to work cooperatively with the community to provide a safe and secure environment by being responsive to the needs of those they serve.

State Police

In January 1918, Golden was chosen as the location for the new state police training center. The state force was a new entity. The country was embroiled in the Great War, and many men from local police and sheriff's departments had joined up or been drafted to fight in France. The men of the state police would provide protection and enforcement in areas throughout every Colorado county. Company No. 1 was under the command of Captain Winfield Grove.

In 1964, Camp George West was proposed as the site for the new law enforcement training center. It remains as the Colorado Law Enforcement Training Academy (CLETA) for new recruits to the Colorado State Patrol. Today, the Colorado State Patrol still uses a portion of the old camp for training and administration.

Camp George West, 2003.

Camp George West was started with the purchase of forty acres from the Denver Rifle Club and served as a rifle range for the Colorado National Guard ca. 1940.

Fire Department

In December 1869, George West issued a call for a fire department in Golden:

> In case of fire, a well organized bucket company would be of great service, and perhaps be the means of saving the town from a destructive conflagration.

A fire marshal, J. C. Remington, was appointed more than a year later, but a fire department was not yet on the agenda of the new town government.

It wasn't until October 2, 1872, that a meeting was held to form the Golden Hook and Ladder Company. C. P. Hoyt was designated as the first foreman, equivalent to the chief. The Golden Hook and Ladder later became the Excelsior Fire Company No. 1. The company had no funds to purchase equipment, so it threw a Thanksgiving Ball and another at New Year's and raised more than $300. In February 1874, it purchased its first apparatus, a "Fire King" engine. The Rescue Hook and Ladder formed on September 23, 1873, and by October had purchased a used hook and ladder apparatus and fifty buckets from St. Joseph, Missouri.

Golden's Board of Trustees established the positions of fire chief and assistant chief in 1874. Five years later, the first designated firehouse was constructed with funding from William Loveland. The Loveland Independent Fire & Hose Company, eventually to become the Golden Volunteer Fire Department, was born. The Central Station was constructed in 1883 next door to the Astor House. In January 1919, the department received its first motorized fire apparatus, a Model "K" International, weighing one and a half tons, with a forty-gallon Champion chemical tank.

Everett Hook and Ladder Company 1885. Top row from left: Pete Reed; John Lomax; middle row: George Vogel; ——— Stevens; V. Van Bramner; F. W. McConkey, chief; Henry Hodges; H. Hinman; F. Fuller; bottom row: L. C. Nixon; Dave Gilbert; Teen Jinachico; J. D. Sivyer, captain; Phil Klatt; William Blatter; John Floyd.

Many things have changed for the fire department since 1879. The Central Station is gone, and since 1961 the department has occupied three bays in the Golden Municipal Center, plus three

additional stations scattered throughout Golden. Fifty-five volunteer firefighters and eight paid staff members respond to an average of three calls per day. The department, now city-funded, is equipped for all forms of rescue from swift water to high-angle, including a helicopter-based team. Seventeen members belong to the Jefferson County Wildland Team, fighting forest fires. Their equipment has improved as well. The department now owns four pumpers, two rescue squads, a brush truck, a tower ladder, a tele-squirt, and a custom-built Attack truck. The new truck was designed by one of Golden's department members. It boasts a 500-gallon water tank, 1,000 feet of hose, and can barrel through four feet of snow. The truck is the only one of its kind in the country.

One thing has not changed: the department's firefighters, those dedicated men and women who man the front lines between the citizens and disaster, are still entirely volunteer. In 1907, when the question was posed as to why Golden did not have a paid department, the response from the *Colorado Transcript* was "because our volunteer boys do such good work that the city authorities have never considered the question." Some things never change.

Churches

The West's seemingly "rough-and-ready" approach to life often gave easterners an exceedingly distorted view of life on the frontier. That notion prompted an 1860 edition of a Kansas Territory newspaper to declare: "There was no Sunday west of Junction City (Kansas) and no God west of Salina (Kansas)." While it is true that days of the week sometimes held little meaning for the mountain man, miner and itinerant trader, within the towns and settlements of the West, it was a very different scene. The "civilizing influences" generally arrived on the heels of the miners and fortune seekers. Shortly after founding, most settlements could be assured the founding of at least one church, a school, and some form of law enforcement. While Golden had and has many churches, space only permits a brief review of some of her pioneer churches.

Golden Fire Department, 2002. From left, top row: J. J. Risch, Tina Gustafson. Middle row: Kevin Ferry, assistant chief; Robert Burrell, assistant chief; Gerard Lutz; John Bales, chief; Jim Hinkle; Jay McCann; Richard Pretz. Bottom row: Joe Anderson; Rex Engstrom; Doug Holschbach, captain; Kevin Milan, division chief; Aaron Giesick; Jerry Stricker, fire marshal; and Tad Cogan.

Women of the Methodist-Episcopal congregation ca. 1930.

First United Methodist Church (Formerly Methodist-Episcopal Church)

Some twenty-seven days after Golden City was organized as a town company, Reverends Jacob Adriance and W. H. Goode arrived in town. They were acting as missionaries for the Kansas-Nebraska Conference. The first service was held on July 17, 1859, in a gambling tent owned by the Ford brothers, allegedly using whiskey barrels as seats. Adriance would later write in his journal that he felt he was "a strange man in a strange country with strange people." These observations were based on his missionary work throughout the area in towns where people gambled seven days a week and shootings were not uncommon.

Since most early-day preachers were circuit riders, a church structure was not immediately necessary. Services were held in available halls, homes, or tents. The first building utilized by the Methodist Church was a log structure at present-day 12th and Jackson Streets. When a larger sanctuary was required in 1868, a brick structure was erected at 14th Street and Washington Avenue. It cost $3,045 to build and was used until 1903. By the 1960s, a larger church was needed; the old, heavily remodeled brick church was no longer feasible. The congregation relocated in 1962 to a 24,000-square-foot edifice at 15th and Ford Streets. The longest continually worshipping Methodist congregation in Colorado also enjoys the distinction of having the oldest Sunday school program as well. It was founded in 1860.

First Baptist Church

In summer 1863, Reverend William Whitehead gathered sixteen people into the top floor of Loveland's Hall to hold the first Baptist service in Golden. The attendees came predominantly from the Barber, Lakes, Huntsman, Snodgrass, and Casto families, a veritable social register of the day. The following January, the congregation incorporated so the church could hold property. Two years later, on August 5, 1866, almost to the day of the congregation's third anniversary, the first sanctuary was dedicated at 12th and Jackson Streets. In the spirit of community, both the Methodist and Episcopal congregations were allowed to hold services in the church until their buildings were completed.

William Austin Hamilton Loveland arrived in Golden just ten days after George West, in June 1859. A successful businessman and a visionary, Loveland opened the first mercantile in Golden and was instrumental in bringing the railroad to the area.

William Austin Hamilton Loveland.

William Loveland offered to donate a bell if the town would add a tower to house it. Tower construction began in July 1867. But disaster nearly befell the bell. Coming by ox team from a foundry in Boston, the caravan was waylaid by Indians. One man and an ox were killed, but the bell arrived in Golden unscathed. Fate was not yet finished with the church. In February 1883, a freakish windstorm hit the city and blew off the church roof; the subsequent snow damaged the ceiling and plasterwork. But the sanctuary was repaired by September, and the church continued to grow.

In 1943, the congregation withdrew from the Northern Baptist Convention and joined the Conservative Baptists of America. In 1960, ground was broken for a new building at 19th Street and Washington Avenue. The pioneer bell was moved and installed proudly between three crosses on the front lawn of the church. And the oldest continuously worshipping Baptist congregation in Colorado still worships in its second sanctuary.

The First Baptist Church's congregation was formed in 1863 and the church building completed in 1866 at 2nd (now 12th) and Jackson Streets. The sign on the front door ca. 1960 announces that the church is moving.

The First Baptist Church ca. 1970. Current location is on Washington Avenue.

St. Joseph's Catholic Church was originally located in downtown Golden but was demolished in the 1970s. The church moved to its current location, adjacent to the Golden Cemetery, in 1986.

St. Joseph's Catholic Church, April 2004.

St. Joseph's Catholic Church

In 1859, Father Joseph Machebeuf arrived in the Territory to conduct the first Roman Catholic Mass in Golden. At the time, there were reportedly only two Catholic families in town, but many other residents came to enjoy the music and fellowship provided by a choir that Machebeuf had brought in from Denver. On May 19, 1867, St. Joseph's first chapel was dedicated. It was situated at approximately 14th and Ford Streets on a 300-by-600-foot lot donated by Judge Jonas Johnson. Both of the Catholic families had donated $100 toward its construction. Machebeuf left Golden and later became the first Roman Catholic bishop of Denver.

The small structure served the ever-growing Golden parish until 1899, when a cornerstone was laid for a new church. The brick structure, completed in 1901, used 75,000 Golden-made pressed bricks and boasted a ninety-three-foot bell tower replete with a gold cross. The structure cost an impressive $10,000 to build. A "basement" church was added across from the brick structure in 1958 to accommodate the burgeoning congregation.

In 1873, St. Joseph's had acquired a plot of land in South Golden for a Catholic cemetery. By the 1960s, the land became an extension of the church's activities. A school opened on the site in 1966. By the 1980s, the congregation of St. Joseph's had outgrown its structure in central

Golden. The old church had been sold to Coors Brewing Company in 1964 and demolished to make way in the 1970s for a parking lot. There was nowhere for the church to expand within the limits of downtown Golden. In the 1980s, the decision was made to move operations to the cemetery and school site. The graves were relocated and ground broken for a new church. The structure was dedicated in 1986 at 969 Ulysses Street, where it still serves the spiritual needs of Golden area Catholics.

Calvary Episcopal Church

The first recorded Episcopal service in Golden was the solemnization of the marriage of the Boston Company's Mark Blunt to Margella Clay on February 5, 1860. The service was conducted by Justice of the Peace James MacDonald; George West gave away the bride. A service was held by itinerant preacher Right Reverend Joseph C. Talbot in August 1861.

The founding of Calvary Episcopal Church did not come until Bishop George Randall sent out a rector, Reverend William Lynd, for Golden City in 1867. Three lots were secured, as well as the promise of $1,000 toward construction of the brick church. The *Colorado Transcript* reported:

> It is proposed to erect a fine building that will be an honor to the society and an ornament to the town. There are many Episcopalians here who will be rejoiced to have a church of their own particular faith to attend regularly. (April 17, 1867)

George West, owner of the *Transcript*, is listed on the early vestry of the church, as were William Loveland and Edward Berthoud. In biographies of Berthoud, it is noted that while he was never a confirmed member of the church, he did attend services regularly when in town. When sermons ran long, Berthoud reportedly would take out his large Swiss watch and wind it.

Calvary Episcopal is the only pioneer church in Golden that remains at its original location. The cornerstone was laid at the southwest corner of present-day 13th and Arapahoe Streets, and while larger now, the church remains in the same spot. Many contractors and artists had a role in constructing the Gothic building. Millikin and Lee, builders of the first Jefferson County Courthouse, did the woodwork; Charles Smith, Simon Bales, and Manuel Smith did the plasterwork; and George Morrison made the stone baptismal font. Additions were made in 1903 and in 1954. In 1998, a new building phase began at the church.

Interior of Calvary Episcopal Church.

First Presbyterian Church

An organizational meeting of residents interested in forming a Presbyterian church was held on March 7, 1870, under the guidance of Reverend Sheldon Jackson. Early meetings and services were held in the Methodist Church and the Baptist Church. E. T. Osborne was elected and ordained as the first elder of the church. Mrs. William Loveland was the first non-charter member to be baptized into the congregation.

On June 16, 1872, the congregation dedicated its first building, located at the corner of 15th Street and Washington Avenue. The twenty-six-by-fifty-foot Gothic edifice could hold 200 parishioners. Several renovations were carried out over the years, including adding a bell tower, a manse, a kitchen, and a fellowship room. Eventually, though, the church was too small to accommodate the burgeoning congregation. A new sanctuary was dedicated in 1957 at South Golden Road and 16th Street, and the beautiful red brick building and manse were adapted into the Foothills Art Center.

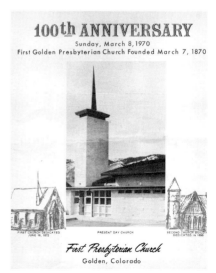

Bulletin, First Presbyterian Church.

Faith Lutheran Church, 2004.

Swedish Lutheran Bible, 1876.

Faith Lutheran Church

The origins of the present-day Faith Lutheran Church actually hark back to the Christian Grace Swedish Lutheran congregation that worshipped in Golden during the nineteenth century. That church was founded in 1873 and remained active until 1930. Dwindling membership forced it to disband, and Golden was without an active Lutheran congregation until 1960.

On October 16, 1960, a group of 176 members of the Lutheran faith met at the Seventh-Day Adventist Church in South Golden. The group laid out a building plan, and on February 5, 1961, the new Faith Lutheran Church was dedicated at 17701 W. 16th Avenue. The first structure was a two-story worship center with a fellowship hall. The second phase, completed in 1975, included seven classrooms, a narthex, offices, and a workroom. The third and final phase, completed in 1987, added a new worship space to the structure

Library

The Territorial Legislature created the first Colorado library in 1867. Edward Berthoud served as librarian. Books could be checked out for ten cents each and retained between ten days and six weeks, depending on where the patron resided. The library was open from 7 p.m. to 9 p.m. each evening except Sunday. When the Legislature moved to Denver, the library went with it.

The effort to found a public library in Golden was spearheaded by four local organizations: the Fortnightly Club, the Bay View Club, the Progressive Club, and the Thursday Musicale. Through their fundraising efforts, in 1914 they were able to purchase property on 13th Street and improve the existing building on the site. Originally, it was a city-funded endeavor, receiving $500 annually during the 1920s. The Monday Evening Club, a local men's group, tried to generate more support for the library and lobbied Jefferson County to get involved, but the county was not yet ready to assume responsibility for it. While not profitable, the library was certainly popular. In 1926, it recorded 4,000 books checked out and added sixty-one new books to the collection. This had increased dramatically by 1955 when the library recorded 13,062 books checked out and 165 new titles added.

In 1961, the library became part of the nine-year-old Jefferson County Public Library system. For a time, it was housed in Golden's city building. But in 1970, a new facility constructed specifically for the library was opened for business next to the city building on 10th Street. In 1996, the library took over the larger building to its west, the former Golden Recreation Center. With that move, it more than doubled its size.

At the turn of the twenty-first century, the Golden Public Library was already in need of expansion because of its rapid growth. In 2002, it recorded an amazing 181,362 visitors. In the same year, it added approximately 13,000 books, CDs, videos, and other media to its collection. It recorded 274,579 items circulated. In the near future, the community can expect to see the library once again stretch its walls to meet the needs of Golden residents.

Golden Public Library interior, 2004.

Clubs

Ever the philosopher and town booster, the *Colorado Transcript* observed on January 23, 1900:

> *In the list of people who injure a town are: First, those who go out of town to do their shopping; second, those who are opposed to improvements; third, those who prefer a quiet town to one of vim and enterprise; fourth, those who imagine they own the town; fifth, those who deride public-spirited men; sixth, those who oppose every movement that does not originate with them; seventh, those who oppose every movement that does not appear to benefit them; eighth, those who seek to injure the credit or reputation of individuals. Take an inventory of yourself and see if you are included in the list.*

Progressive Club ca. 1900. Pictured here are: Mrs. Lucretia DeFrance, C. P. Hoyt, W. G. Smith, ——— Arrowsmith, D. W. Garrison, ——— Jameson, D. C. Crawford, and J. H. Brown.

Since 1859, Golden has hosted many organizations that have all contributed immeasurably to the growth and success of the town. Some were social clubs, others were service organizations, and still others centered on growth and development. The groups highlighted here are just a few of the many who have graced Golden's history and continue to do so.

Golden Civic Foundation

The Golden Civic Foundation was incorporated on April 14, 1970, under the Colorado Non-Profit Act. It was founded by several business owners who realized that Golden had many needs for which tax revenues and other public funds were simply not available. The first Board of Directors included F. A. Foss, F. J. Pattridge, W. G. Brown, C. Goudge, and R. W. Todd. More than twenty-five other individuals have served on the foundation's Board of Directors.

The purpose of the Golden Civic Foundation is to raise funds for the betterment of Golden. The foundation raises its capital through private means as well as an annual dinner and auction. The funds are distributed to charitable and cultural organizations in Golden and are also used to make improvements to various public properties. In the past, the foundation has also acquired under-utilized properties to sell to organizations that will develop them to enhance the beauty and economic vitality of the city.

To date, the foundation has contributed more than $600,000 to capital projects and another $600,000 to charitable and cultural organizations. Among these projects are the revitalization of the junior high school building into the American Alpine Center, the public art projects, and improvements at nearly every museum in Golden.

Grand Army of the Republic (GAR)

The Grand Army of the Republic was established in 1866 at Decatur, Illinois, by Union Army and Navy veterans of the American Civil War. The two women's auxiliary groups were known as the Women's Relief Corps and the Ladies of the GAR. Their purpose was to preserve the memory of their fallen comrades, to strengthen the bonds of comradeship, to provide aid to soldier's widows, orphans, and handicapped veterans, and to fight for pensions and other benefits for veterans. The GAR was ultimately responsible for the adoption of Memorial Day. Annual encampments throughout the country gave the veterans a chance to catch up and swap war stories.

Because Golden had many Civil War veterans living in town, a post was established on May 17, 1879. The Theodore H. Dodd Post No. 7, later Post No. 3, had nineteen charter members. Among the first members were Lieutenant Colonel T. J. Capps, Captain Edward Berthoud, Captain George West, and Corporal A. D. Jameson. The Golden Post held its final meeting in 1927 when ranks had thinned to eight members. The last national encampment was held in April 1949, with only sixteen surviving members nationwide. The organization now exists only as crumbling documents in museums and memorials in cemeteries nationwide.

Fortnightly Club

In September 1886, a group of socially prominent Golden ladies organized a study club called the Addison Chautauquan Circle, which was destined to become the oldest continuously operating women's club in Colorado.

Initially, membership was limited to fifteen women, with additional honorary and associate members. In the twenty-first century, membership is limited to twenty-five with several associate memberships.

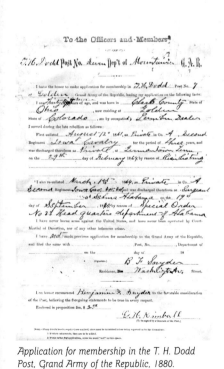

Application for membership in the T. H. Dodd Post, Grand Army of the Republic, 1880.

The first meeting of the club was held at the home of Mrs. C. C. Welch. Eleven women gathered to begin the Chautauqua course. Their first course of study, completed by seven of them, included geology, chemistry, astronomy, English literature, American literature, British history, American history, zoology, history of the medieval church, physiology, Roman history and literature, Greek history and literature, political economy, and physics.

Following the completion of this first study course, the club was reorganized as a Macaulay club, studying the British historian's works for the subsequent three years. Then, in 1893, the club was again reorganized as the Golden Fortnightly Club. In December 1894, it was admitted to the General Federation of Women's Clubs and in 1895 became a charter member of the State Federation of Colorado Women's Clubs.

Over the years, the club has worked on various service projects as well as study courses. During World Wars I and II, members helped roll bandages and make clothing for the Red Cross. They have sponsored the Campfire Girls, the Golden Music Week, and the Jefferson Symphony Orchestra. Today, the organization exists primarily as a study club.

Lucretia DeFrance, charter member of the Golden Fortnightly Club.

Members of the Golden Fortnightly Club, 2004: Genie deLuise, Dorothy Crawford, Barbara Crane, and Ann Moore.

Mount Lookout Chapter of the Daughters of the American Revolution dedicating the marker commemorating the site of the Boston Company building in Parfet Park. September 2, 1927.

Daughters of the American Revolution (DAR)

On June 15, 1923, seventeen women met to found a chapter of the Daughters of the American Revolution. The list of attendees reads like a list of who's who in Golden: Paddleford, Read, Warren, Coolbaugh, Dier, Jameson, and Fitch. These women, all descendants of patriots in the American Revolution, were dedicated to the principles on which the DAR is founded, among them historic preservation. The chapter was named Mount Lookout in honor of the mountain to Golden's west. Its first regent was Mrs. L. D. Roberts.

The Daughters wasted no time getting involved in preservation activities. Chief among them was the Boston Company building, which had fallen into complete disrepair. The chapter hoped to save it from demolition and found a museum on the first floor. However, the man who purchased the building moved it from Parfet Park, then demolished it on its new site in Pleasant View. The chapter felt that at the very least, the location of Golden's first permanent building should be marked. And, on September 2, 1927, it placed a stone from Clear Creek on the spot in Parfet Park bearing a brass plaque denoting the significance of the site.

Mount Lookout Chapter of the Daughters of the American Revolution planting a tree on Arbor Day 2004.

Additional preservation efforts continued, with the largest coming in 1953. Since World War II, the collection of the Jefferson County Pioneer Museum had been in storage in the basement of the County Courthouse. The Daughters offered to reopen the museum in the second-floor District Courtroom of the courthouse. The county agreed, and with funds as well as help from many quarters, the museum reopened on February 22, 1954. Since that time, the Daughters have continued their work with the museum, seeing it though two subsequent homes, a change of ownership, and several staff changes. Today, the Daughters still provide Board members and volunteers to help the museum in its daily operations. The chapter as a whole remains very active in veterans' events, Arbor Day work, fundraising efforts, and genealogy.

Golden Lions of Lions International

Over the years, Golden has had many organizations dedicated to the betterment of the community. Today, one of the most visible is the Golden Lions Club. Founded in 1943, the club and its activities have become an integral part of the Golden scene. The Lions received their charter on February 4, 1943, at a ceremony in Golden High School. Twenty-seven members comprised the first membership roster. Membership has grown to more than sixty civic-minded individuals.

Golden Kiwanis Club ca. 1940. Back row, from left: ———, Walt Koch, Dick White, Father Wogan, ———. Front row: Clyde Gregory, ———, Chuck Herron.

Lions Park, 2003.

The Lions became involved in war work immediately. Initially involved with the local blood bank, the club eventually formed its own, placing second in 1944 among statewide Lions clubs for collecting 446 pints of blood. The blood bank operation continued after World War II, with donations made to the Red Cross. Subsequently, the Lions began sponsoring local children's groups such as the Golden Melodears, the Boy Scouts, and the Camp Fire Girls. Among their numerous civic projects is the "comfort station," constructed in 1955 in Parfet Park, followed in 1994 by construction of the "Taj Ma Stall," a restroom facility, on 12th Street next to the Astor House Museum.

Over the years, the Lions constructed playgrounds, picnic tables, and baseball dugout covers, and they have been instrumental in the funding of many more projects throughout Golden. The first annual Chili Supper was held on November 2, 1956, and remains an annual event in Golden and one of the Lions' most widely known fundraising events. Ground was broken for Lions Park in 1973. It remains as one of the family-favorite parks in the area. It is also the site for the Lions' annual Fourth of July community picnic and fireworks event. Recent activities include the purchase of a monitoring unit for the Foothills Ambulance Service, donations to Leader Dogs for the Blind, and contributions to the New York Police and Fire Departments following the events of September 11, 2001.

Success had so taken hold in Golden that George West observed on July 31, 1867:

> Between the bright prospects of Golden City and the rapidly growing town of Cheyenne, our Denver friends are getting in a pucker. We hope they will survive the growth of these two thrifty cities....Progress is the order of the day.
>
> George West
> Colorado Transcript

Whether for good or bad, Golden did not supersede Denver in size or industry. The town continues to grow gradually. Rather than seeking to be the largest or most progressive, Golden seeks, at least in the early years of the twenty-first century, to be very good at what it is—a small town with a quaint western flair.

Top: Taken from Lookout Mountain, this hand-colored photograph shows Golden nestled between the heights of North and South Table Mountains ca. 1915.

Middle: Over the last century and a half, Golden has grown significantly yet remains confined by the mountains that border it, 2003.

Far Left: *The Metropolitan Barbershop. From left to right: Clive "Shorty" Straight, Gibb Reeves, and Elmer Grazier, ca. 1920.*

Left: *The Sportsman Barbershop retains much of the charm of its predecessors.*

The acclaimed Fossil Trace Golf Course provides a challenge to golfers combined with incredible views of the Colorado Front Range.

Left: The weather forecast for 1913 was for snow, followed by snow, with a chance of snow.

Above: Gary Christopher Gunnison, an early visitor.

Below: Clear Creek History Park October 2004

Top: *This 1873 image shows the Golden House, the Episcopal Church, and South School under construction.*

Above: *Calvary Episcopal Church is the only pioneer church in Golden to still occupy its original site.*

Right: *Constructed in 1913, the National Guard Armory now graces the site once occupied by the Golden House.*

Built by Nankieval and Jones, the building at 10th Street and Washington Avenue once housed the Caleb Elsworth Parfet Grocery, ca. 1895. C. E. Parfet sold a variety of goods, including imported fine French white china. Margaret Parfet hand-painted the china and edged each plate with gold she had panned from Clear Creek.

Restored to the time when E. E. Stewart owned the building, it is now occupied by several small businesses. While the Indian painted on the side of the building has become a local landmark, it only first appeared in the 1950s.

BRIDGE LOAD LIMIT

20 HEAD OF HORNED CATTLE
OR
20 HEAD OF HORSES OR MULES
OR
60 HEAD OF HOGS
OR
100 HEAD OF SHEEP
AT A
PACE NOT TO EXCEED A WALK

PENALTY FOR OVERLOAD
NOT LESS THAN $50
NOT MORE THAN $100

HISTORIC SIGN FROM GOLDEN CITY
ORDINANCE #28, 1883

Right: *One of Golden's earliest ordinances concerning the bridge over Clear Creek on Washington Avenue is still enforced.*

Below: *The Golden Visitors Center and Chamber of Commerce work tirelessly to promote Golden through a series of events throughout the year.*

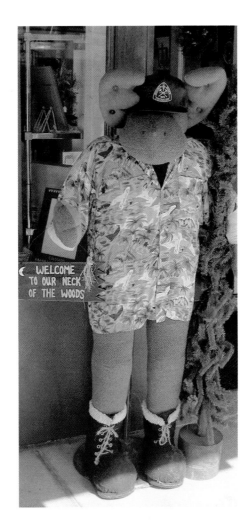

Far left: The Ford Street bridge serves cars, pedestrians, and the occasional wildlife.

Left: There's always a friendly face to welcome visitors to Golden.

Below: Golden's history is a history of the lives and activities of people. The valley still attracts people seeking to capture the "golden spirit."

Right: Dr. Kelly and his son operated one of Golden's downtown pharmacies at the turn of the century. Their Italianate-style home is a hallmark of the 12th Street Historic District.

Below: The new Canyon Point development occupies much of the north end of Golden.

While deep snows fall occasionally, most Golden winters are marked by brief snows followed by bright sun and picturesque views.

Above: *This 1873 image of downtown Golden shows the Avenue Hotel, the Everett Building (under construction), and the Loveland Building.*

Below: *Washington Avenue 1995.*

Vanover Park on Clear Creek looking north to North Table Mountain ca. 2004.

The Golden Opera House opened its doors on October 26, 1879, above the local pool hall, which is now the Ace Hi Tavern.

Chapter Five

How The West Plays

For Christmas 1859, William Loveland threw a gala ball at his unfinished building on Washington Avenue. Fifty couples attended, and music was provided by McDuffee and Ackley. This grand event would be succeeded by a ball or party nearly every week for decades. While there may not have been many residents, the few who resisted the draw of the gold fields were always amenable to a good time. Entertainment of all sorts has graced Golden at one time or another, ranging from stage plays to "play ball!" The little town has never lacked for something to do.

Pioneer women traveling to the west did not leave fashion behind. A silk gown similar to this may have been worn at Golden's first formal ball, ca. 1860.

Theater and Music

Golden's first recorded theatrical event was in the last week of December 1859. Mademoiselle Haydee and her sisters performed several musical selections at the Jefferson House, a local boardinghouse. They were well received, and the Misses Haydee would perform several more times. Theater continued to be a significant part of Golden's civic scene, though not without reservation on the part of some community members. In June 1867, the following admonishment regarding theater appeared in the *Colorado Transcript*:

> If it is potent for evil, let us make it so for good. Its managers are our servants, and will introduce into it the spirit which they think will please us most... Let the language be the most chaste. Let heroes fall when they become vicious. Let them show that if we would be honored we must be good. Let our youth leave the playhouse with a new impetus to great and noble deeds.

For better or worse, theater was here to stay, and in 1879 the Golden Opera House was constructed on Washington Avenue. It provided entertainment ranging from theater productions to dances and dinners well into the twentieth century. The Ace-Hi Tavern now occupies the first floor of the building.

The 1887 cast of "The Oratorio of Esther the Beautiful" at the Golden Opera House.

Founded in 1929, the Golden Thespians remained an active part of the Golden theater scene for decades. On average, they produced two plays per year, performed in the Colorado School of Mines' Guggenheim Hall. In 1971, they were permitted to take over the old site of St. Joseph's Catholic Church on East Street and renovate it into a performance space. Theater members cleaned and repainted it, and a Boulder-based theater company donated seats. Renamed the Cathedral Playhouse, it opened with performances of "Send Me No Flowers," a comedy by Norman Barasch and Carroll Moore, in October 1971. The theater closed in the late 1970s when the old church structure was sold to Coors Brewing Company and torn down.

The set of "The Elephant Man" at the Miner's Alley Playhouse, 2003.

Golden went through a theater dry spell until the 2003 arrival of the Miner's Alley Playhouse. Seeking a larger space and more control over their operations, the former Morrison Theatre moved to Golden and renovated a space above Foss Drug on Washington Avenue and 13th Street in spring 2003. The theater group's first performance in its new space was "The Elephant Man."

Movies came to Golden in 1908. The Electric Theater on Jackson Street played silent films. Other theaters such as the Pixie and the Golden Theater opened and closed throughout downtown Golden between the early 1900s and the 1920s. The first theater to show "talkies" was the Gem. The film was "The Donovan Case," and it opened in June 1929. The Gem building still stands on the southeast corner of 13th Street and Washington Avenue, though today it houses retail and office space instead of a movie screen.

Everywhere people travel, they bring their music with them, and Golden was no exception. Bands were formed by many of the clubs and schools. The Woodman of the World, a fraternal life insurance society, had a marching band, as did the State Industrial School and the State School of Mines. Mines also boasted a mandolin club. At the turn of the century, Golden hosted a ragtime dance at the opera house. Local musicians performed, including George Kimball on E-flat coronet, Gordon Davis on clarinet, A. G. Christiansen on slide trombone, and L. B. West on bass drum.

The Golden Gem Building, 2003.

Released in 1935, "Devil Dogs of the Air" starred James Cagney and Pat O'Brien. "Scotland Yard" was made in 1941 and starred Edwin Gwenn as Inspector Cork. Golden Gem, ca. 1941.

Woodman of the World Band. A fraternal family-member organization, operating chiefly in the Western states, Woodman of the World was founded in Denver in 1890. It has become a well-known member insurance company. Pictured fifth from the left in the front row is George M. Kimball, who ran the Colorado Transcript after George West's retirement.

The Golden Civic Orchestra began as a small community ensemble in 1953. Known now as the Jefferson Symphony Orchestra, it has grown into a well-respected ninety-five-piece community orchestra in its truest sense. One of the few volunteer orchestras in the Front Range, the JSO continues the tradition of bringing classical and pops concerts to Jefferson County.

The Rock Rest Lodge is still a popular watering hole.

Even during Prohibition, Golden found ways to have fun. The Lava Lane and the Rock Rest were two of the dance halls within driving, or streetcar, distance. The Lava Lane, high atop Castle Rock, was a whites-only establishment offering a tame version of the 1920s hot jazz sound. It burned down in 1927 under suspicious circumstances, but the stairs and some remnants of the building's footings still remain on top of the mountain.

The Rock Rest for a time was owned by legendary jazzman George Morrison. He sold his share of the Rock Rest in the mid-1920s, having been pressured out by local Ku Klux Klansmen. The club still sits on South Golden Road, playing popular music from the 1980s and 1990s.

Jefferson County sought to exert some control over the establishments by charging a $25 annual license fee to any hall where soft drinks were served. Despite the fee and the continual raids in search of alcohol, many dance halls managed to serve their patrons something a bit stronger than Coca-Cola.

The Castle Rock Mountain Railway carries passengers toward the Lava Lane Dance Hall atop Castle Rock, ca. 1915.

Cultural Pursuits

The headline read, "Museum for Golden May Be Started." The date was February 24, 1938. This was the first mention of a museum for Golden. Prior to that time, a lack of both space and supervision were cited as the reasons why one had not been started. Space became available in the North School, and the federal Works Progress Administration (WPA) had funds to provide supervision. *The Colorado Transcript* was certain that travelers to Golden would be happy to pay ten to twenty-five cents to view pioneer artifacts, as they were used to paying for such a privilege in other cities, however, once approved the admission to the museum was free. The Jefferson County Pioneer Museum was an instant success. Families from throughout the area donated hundreds of items to the new venture. The newspaper suggested that the ladies overseeing the museum dress in pioneer costumes and serve tea on Sunday afternoons to create a special attraction for visitors.

The North School, located on 6th Street and Washington Avenue, was the first home of the Pioneer Museum.

The Pioneer Museum closed down during World War II, and many of the artifacts were returned to the families. In 1953, the Mount Lookout Chapter of the Daughters of the American Revolution took it on as a historic preservation project and reopened the museum in 1954. Since then, the Golden Pioneer Museum has had several homes and continues to grow. The museum houses approximately 10,000 artifacts including photographs, books, clothing, and furniture. The 2,500-volume research library contains both genealogy and local history items. The annual program schedule includes activities for all ages.

Seth Lake came to Golden during the 1860s. He constructed a hotel on 2nd Street (now 12th Street) called the Lake House. His second endeavor was the Astor House, built in 1867 to house territorial legislators. The name was to suggest that it was as grand as any eastern hotel. The boardinghouse was rescued from demolition in the 1970s. It had fallen into severe disrepair and was slated to be leveled to make way for a parking lot when a group of concerned citizens formed the Golden Landmarks Association and worked diligently to purchase and restore the

The building that now houses the Golden Pioneer Museum was built in 1969 by the Jefferson County Library System and housed the Golden Branch until 1996.

Jack Pearce purchased the cabin in the background at right and moved it to his land in Golden Gate Canyon.

Before it was moved to Clear Creek History Park, the Jack Pearce cabin sat atop Drew Hill. The cabin is now a point of interest at Clear Creek History Park.

Built in 1867 of native sandstone, the Astor House was a convenient place for the territorial legislators to stay while in session. In 1867, patrons paid $1.50 per day or $4.50 per week for room and board.

The Astor House was destined to become a parking lot before it was rescued from demolition by Golden citizens in 1972. The historic structure is now a museum that interprets the time period 1867 to 1908.

Foothills Art Center, 2004.

boardinghouse. It is now a museum interpreting the latter half of the nineteenth century. Its sister site is the Clear Creek History Park, a living-history enclave on the banks of Clear Creek showcasing life ways and buildings rescued from Golden Gate Canyon.

Incorporated in 1968, the Foothills Art Center occupies the impressive sandstone structure that once housed the First Presbyterian Church in downtown Golden. From 1872 until 1958, the church held services in the building before moving to a larger structure. For a time, the building was home to various community cultural programs, classes, and art shows. The art center has hosted many wonderful exhibits over the decades, ranging from watercolor to sculpture. Classes and lectures are just a few of its additional public offerings.

In 1990, the Rocky Mountain Quilt Museum opened its doors with a collection of one hundred quilts donated by its founder, Eugenia Mitchell. The museum now boasts a collection of more than 250 quilts including the "Golden History Quilt," which depicts the history of Golden from 1859 to 1913. The museum is housed in a building that is new to Golden's skyline. The brick structure sits adjacent to a *Colorado Transcript* facility.

Trains came to Golden in the 1870s. Theirs and Golden's history are forever joined, thanks to William Loveland, who had a vision of Golden as a railroad center. That vision never came to pass, but Golden does enjoy being home to one of the foremost railroad museums in the nation. The Colorado Railroad Museum, located on Golden's eastern edge near the former enclave of Arapahoe Bar, was established in 1959 to preserve for future generations a tangible record of Colorado's railroad era, particularly the state's pioneering narrow gauge mountain railroads. The fifteen-acre site boasts a five-stall roundhouse complete with inspection pit and a machine shop where restoration on its many engines and train cars is conducted. More than seventy railroad exhibits guide the visitor through the fascinating history of railroading in Colorado.

The Colorado Railroad Museum dedicated the Cornelius W. Hauck Restoration Facility/ Roundhouse on July 15, 2000. The five-stall roundhouse is a composite design and now houses the museum's machine shop, welding, and wood shops.

The Colorado Central Roundhouse ca. 1880.

Driving the Lariat Trail up Lookout Mountain was a popular Sunday activity in the early twentieth century ca. 1915.

Just Fun Stuff

Entertainment in Golden has not always been limited to intellectual pursuits. Since the early days, Goldenites have always been ready for just plain fun. Parties, balls, and auto races have long held the interest of residents.

This notice ran in the October 26, 1898, issue of the *Colorado Transcript*. Most parties and balls were advertised through the society listing, inviting the entire town to the event.

Some of the most popular balls given at the Golden Opera House were those sponsored by the Golden Volunteer Fire Department. Often referred to as "smokers," these dinner-dances were intended to raise money for equipment and other needs of the department. Ads for the events were always prominent in the society column, as was the post-dance coverage.

Automobile spectacles began almost as soon as the car arrived in Golden. In 1927, the *Denver Post* sponsored "The Last Leap of Leaping Lena." This was the first time cars, or "Tin Lizzies," were pushed off the top of Castle Rock over Golden. It was quite a spectacle, according to those who witnessed it on February 13, 1927. The Golden

Ye Golden Tyme

Ye are one and all invited to meet ye Spukes of ye Olden Tyme on Hallowe'en of 1898, and join in ye eatables, which are to be had for the small sum of two shillings for the coming and one eating. Laughter and no end of fun, in the which all ye young and ye old can hold forth without charge. If ye appear at ye Golden Door (Opera House) with ye invite, in becoming attire of ye olden style, ye can get in when curfew rings.

With respect.

Mesdames Prudence Gayton
Mahittable Wise
Patience Amour
Ye Committee

The Spring House on Lookout Mountain Drive, Denver Mountain Parks, ca. 1920.

Hill Climb up Lookout Mountain was another popular auto sport. It received recognition from the Sports Club of America, which enabled the town to open the event to 5,000 sports car drivers. Neither event is held in Golden anymore, and the only auto spectacles are community-oriented car shows that take place throughout the year in downtown Golden and at Heritage Square, and an auto rally over Lariat Loop held each June.

The ruins of the Lookout Mountain Drive Springhouse can still be seen.

Magic Mountain

Golden was very nearly home to a Disneyesque theme park at its southern edge. In the early 1950s, C. V. Wood, an architect for Disney, arrived with a plan to build a series of parks across the country, similar in design and scope to the recently opened Disneyland in Anaheim, California. Walt Disney, however, was not amenable to the plan, and he fired Wood and all his associates who were employed by the company. Renderings of the proposed park detail myriad themes including a frontier area, a future area, and a pirate ship. The park opened on a limited basis in 1957, but the bank foreclosed on the property due to extreme financial mismanagement. It reopened in 1970 as Heritage Square. The park is now a small collection of shops, rides, and a melodrama theater. While Heritage Square is not precisely what Wood had envisioned, perhaps it is more suited to the small town environment Golden and the surrounding area.

Magic Mountain stock offering portfolio.

Magic Mountain reopened as Heritage Square in 1970 with shops, rides, and a theater, as shown here, ca. 2003.

Magic Mountain opened in 1957 but soon closed, causing many Goldenites to lose their investments in the project.

Fun in the Golden Sun

Colorado is known for being an outdoor enthusiast's paradise. Since the mid-1800s, mountain climbers, hikers, and sportsmen of all types have found adventure, challenge, and fun in the state's beautiful mountains. Golden is no exception. Its position, nestled firmly against not only the Rocky Mountain foothills but also North and South Table Mountains, affords it the best of many worlds, for here one can partake of four seasons of outdoor fun and games.

Women enjoyed a variety of sports, including tennis, during Golden's early days, ca. 1900.

Football

Football came to Golden in the 1890s with the formation of the State School of Mines team. It joined teams already in action from the Denver Athletic Club. In those early days, the collegiate teams often played semipro teams from the region. It didn't matter much to the Mines boys because they had a tremendous powerhouse team from the start. In their November 22, 1890, game against the University of Colorado (CU) Buffaloes, Mines trounced the Buffs 103 to 0. CU fullback Conrad Blohm said of the loss, "It wasn't so bad, considering." This game certainly must have contributed to the already fierce rivalry between the two schools. Devoted CU fans were known to rework the Mines "M" on Mount Zion into a "C"; Mines fans retaliated in various creative and sometimes explosive ways.

In 1893 Mines, CU, the University of Denver, Colorado College, and the Colorado Agricultural College (Colorado State University) formed the Colorado Intercollegiate Athletic Association. It was re-formed in 1909 as the Colorado Faculty Athletic Association, removing a great deal of control over games and schedules from the students and placing it in the hands of the faculty.

Mines continued to enjoy gridiron success into the early twentieth century. In 1906, under coach "Shorty" Ellsworth, they brought home the pennant for the Rocky Mountain Region for the third straight year. Their record was two wins, no losses, and two ties. Second place went to the University of Denver with two wins, two losses, and no ties. CU, Mines' arch rival, finished third with one win, one loss, and one tie.

Mines' boys still battle it out on the gridiron every fall, though with somewhat less success than they had in earlier years. Emphasis strongly shifted to more academic pursuits as the twentieth century progressed. One thing has not changed—the rivalry between the Colorado School of Mines and the University of Colorado at Boulder remains legendary, if not occasionally hazardous.

Colorado School of Mines vs. the University of Colorado, November 28, 1907. The championship football game was won by the School of Mines, with a score of 5 to 4.

Seventh and eighth grade North School Baseball Team. Back row, left to right: William Golightly, John Walker, Harold Simmons, Wilbur Shephard, George Allen, Oscar Johnson. Front Row: Eddie Hoffmaster, Carl Anderson, Ernie VanWinkle, Raymond Williams, George Goldberg. Team mascot Cliff Buzzert sits in front, ca. 1930.

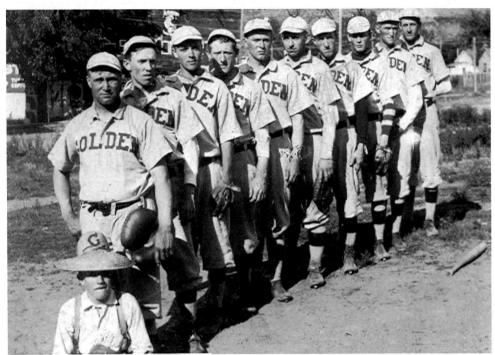

Golden Baseball Team, 1910, from left to right: Hartzell, Dennis Standard, McIntyre, B. Taylor, Ortsier, J. Jeuch, Baird Maughan, and Jones.

Baseball

Baseball, the all-America sport made famous by Abner Doubleday, has deep roots in Colorado. The game came West with the settlers, though the bat was shorter and the ball softer. Historian Duane Smith notes that "Baseball united diverse and often fragmented groups of newly arrived Coloradans." Miners in the mountain camps played it to pass the time on their day off. Union and Confederate soldiers in the field played it to relieve stress. Much of the nation scorned Colorado because baseball games and bicycle races were held on Sundays and were often bet upon.

A fierce rivalry existed between the teams from Denver, Golden, and Central City. The *Rocky Mountain News* reported in 1874: "We are a little impatient for them to commence breaking each other's heads." Indeed, baseball was not the comparatively tame sport we enjoy today. A 1924 *Colorado Transcript* article details the casualty list from a match between Golden and Evergreen: one broken leg, one busted finger, two broken ribs, one strained leg, one fractured toe, and one black eye. Golden beat Evergreen 20 to 6.

Back in the late 1800s and early 1900s, virtually everyone had a team. Golden fielded teams from the volunteer fire department, the State School of Mines, and the city, and in the 1930s Coors Brewing Company sponsored a Negro League team. Both men and women played, though on separate teams that occasionally played each other. One memorable game of note was in August, 1898 between the Goldens (men's team) and the Bloomers (ladies' team). The Goldens beat the Bloomers 10 to 8. The *Transcript* reported:

> *It was a grand sight...to see these big muscular women sliding into the arms of the basemen who were so completely carried away with the novelty of the occasion that they would invariably catch the runners instead of the ball.*

Steve Stevens, owner of the Golden Oldy Cyclery, is often seen riding his high-wheel bicycle throughout the Golden area.

Early on, little care was given to which teams played one another. Today, for example, college teams play only other college teams. Back then, college teams played professional teams, and amateurs often played semipro teams. In 1901, the Mines team beat the Goldens 11 to 5. This practice was stopped early in the twentieth century to reduce injuries and make the games more equitable.

Today in Golden, baseball teams are found at the schools and as an intramural activity for adults and children. The town no longer boasts a semipro team.

Bicycling

Bicycling made its presence known in the area in about 1869. It was almost entirely a man's sport—specifically a wealthy man's sport—until the 1890s when bicycles became more rider-friendly and affordable. Various newspaper accounts note that the velocipedes frightened horses and created a general hazard. Regardless of the cost or hazard, bicycling took a firm grip on Colorado and has not yet let go.

The first recorded bicycle race was on April 6, 1869, between the *Denver Tribune's* Deacon Walker, General Nathan Harris, and "a gentleman from Golden." The men competed for a $100 prize. Harrison won when the others had difficulties with their bikes. Racing became a popular pastime with friendly wagers being the norm. Denver ended up on the wrong side of a national debate concerning racing when it became widely known that Denverites, and probably by

This gentleman's bicycle advertises Morgan & Wright Tires ca. 1900.

Bicycling in Red Rocks, Colorado, ca. 1890.

default Goldenites, preferred holding races on Sundays, a direct violation of the League of American Wheelman's edict. But the races have continued virtually unabated into the twenty-first century.

Newspapers and cyclists throughout the state noted good roads for cycling, the span between Golden and Morrison being particularly appreciated. Recreational cycling clubs sprang up throughout the area such as the Denver Wheel Club and the Denver Athletic Club. Governor Alva Adams, himself an avid cyclist, spearheaded the development of many riding trails throughout the Front Range. By the 1890s, women were also partaking of the fine roads and trails with bikes specially designed for use while wearing a split skirt or bloomer outfit.

But tension between cyclists, pedestrians, and motorists was inevitable, and the *Colorado Transcript* was often vociferous in its hostility toward early cyclists. On November 1, 1899, in an accident report concerning L. J. Fox, the paper reported that the "fiery, untamed bicycle is getting in its vengeful work all around us." So-called "scorchers" and "cyclomaniacs" were targets of special criticism. Scorchers rode in excess of ten miles per hour on public throughways, and cyclomaniacs ruined the experience for all by being excessively dangerous.

The tension between cyclists and noncyclists continues. In the 1980s, the Denver Regional Council of Governments estimated there were well over 600,000 bicycle owners in the metro area. Coupled with nearly one million automobiles, it is bound to create some measure of havoc. Incidents of road rage against cyclists on public roads have increased, with some deaths reported in the metro area. Trails are also a point of contention. Hikers maintain that mountain bikes should not be permitted on trails because they present a hazard. The controversy grew to such a degree that in the mid-1990s, Jefferson County Open Space considered prohibiting cyclists from their mountain trails, including several in the Golden area. The ban has not yet been put in place, possibly because of the economic impact the sport has on the region.

There are approximately 10,000 miles of bike track crisscrossing Colorado. By the mid-1990s, there were an estimated 350 bicycle stores in Colorado. Golden has two. In 1975, Moe Siegel, the founder of Celestial Seasonings Tea Company in Boulder, Colorado, started an annual bike race called the Red Zinger Bicycle Classic. Coors Brewing Company took over the sponsorship in 1980. The Coors International Bike Classic is one of the most popular races in the county. Adding to that are now the Fat Tire Classic, and Ride the Rockies, among others. Bicycling in Colorado is now a $700 million annual industry.

Golf

The Golden Golf Club was organized in August 1930 with forty-eight members, but a site for a course had not yet been selected. A possible location was eighty acres along the Golden-to-Boulder road just east of Golden Gate Canyon. However, Golden's dream of a golf course did not materialize until 2002 with the creation of the Fossil Trace Golf Course.

Fossil Trace, a challenging eighteen-hole, par-72 course, was designed by golf course architect James J. Engh, designer of the Sanctuary Golf Course, Red Hawk Ridge, and Redlands Mesa Golf Course. It is located nowhere near the 1930 proposed location but rather winds around the Lookout Mountain Youth Services Center and through the old Parfet clay mine along U.S. Highway 6. The course, unlike any other in the nation, permits access to preserved fossil sites and boasts interpretive signage with information about the fossils, geology, and historic sites.

Mountain Sports

Letters and postcards dating back to the late 1800s indicate that Golden was a popular spot for tourists to spend a day hiking. It was readily accessible from Denver by train, carriage, or trolley. And hikes from easy to strenuous could be experienced within a day—no camping gear required. Both men and women would scale the heights of Lookout Mountain, Mount Zion, and both of the Table Mountains. Views that ranged from Wyoming to Kansas were afforded

Lookout Mountain Nature Center, 2003.

From its earliest days, tourists arrived in Golden for recreation and relaxation. Hartzell's Place on Lookout Mountain provided a camp ground for those who wished to "rough it."

The American Alpine Club and the Colorado Mountain Club beautifully restored the old junior high school and installed a climbing wall.

the adventurous. Since those early days, an elaborate system of trails has been developed, primarily by locals partaking of the experience but more recently by the Jefferson County Open Space system. Within a twenty-minute drive from Golden, there are 163 miles of hiking trails. Many are open to horses and bicyclists as well.

For the bird watcher or the hiker seeking a less rustic adventure, there is the Lookout Mountain Nature Center. It is part of the Jefferson County Open Space system and offers something for everyone. Visitors can connect with nature on the 110-acre preserve by strolling trails winding through forest and meadow or picnic beneath towering pine trees. Naturalists help visitors discover natural treasures on guided programs. Inside the visitor/nature center, interactive exhibits reveal some of nature's secrets.

Rock climbing has become a popular activity. The basalt heights of North Table Mountain attract technical climbers from throughout Colorado. The cliffs, lit by the bright summer sun, afford the opportunity to scale deep crevices and test one's endurance. There are also less difficult areas for the novice climber.

As if all of that wasn't enough, Golden is the home to the American Alpine Club and the Colorado Mountain Club. Both are housed, along with Colorado Outward Bound, in the old junior high school building, which has been lovingly restored on the exterior and beautifully improved inside. The Alpine Club has one of the most extensive mountaineering libraries in the world with volumes dating back to the 1500s. The clubs offer a wide array of programs for all

Rock climbers scale the rugged cliffs of North Table Mountain.

Hoyt family and friends pose in their bathing costumes ca. 1900.

Whitewater enthusiasts hone their skills on the Clear Creek Kayak Course.

ages, including classes, trips, and a film festival. A museum on the history of mountaineering is forthcoming.

Water Sports

Golden boasts the only championship-caliber kayak course in the Denver area. The Clear Creek Kayak Course, extended through downtown Golden in 2003, has attracted the Eddie Bauer Kayak International event as well as young people in training for the U.S. Junior Olympics. For the more leisurely water sports fan, tubing is also a popular summer activity on Clear Creek.

Golden's newest swimming pool is Splash at Fossil Trace.

If water fun is the desire but braving the chilly waters of Clear Creek is not, then one of Golden's newest attractions might fit the bill. The Splash at Fossil Trace aquatic park offers slides, a leisure pool, water features, and an eight-lane competition pool. It opened in summer 2002.

Flying

If you're not too fond of climbing mountains, then how about sailing off them? As early as the 1930s, people were noticing that Golden was an exceptional spot for taking advantage of the updrafts and air currents produced by its proximity to the mountains. Back then, sports enthusiasts were advocating gliding and sail-planing as the perfect recreational sport. Today, it's paragliding and hang-gliding.

Mount Zion, located just to the west of the city, affords an ideal location for hang-gliding and paragliding. For decades, enthusiasts with a passion for catching the spiraling air thermals have found the skies over Golden to be just the ticket.

Many other sports and forms of entertainment have graced the City of Golden—hockey, basketball, skateboarding, and funiculars, to name a few. Over the years, Golden has become a little town with a lot to do. There are eight museums within its borders and several more close by. These wonderful cultural institutions sponsor a wide array of events and activities to suit every age and interest—including steam engine steam-ups, teas, art classes, summer camps, lectures, and luncheons. Golden boasts the headquarters for such esteemed organizations as the American Alpine Club and Colorado Outward Bound. There are fine theater productions, a dance hall, water sports, and an amusement park in proximity to the downtown. In addition, there are street fairs such as Buffalo Bill Days, a farmer's market, a juried Fine Arts Fest, and a holiday celebration like no other. Whatever your interest, you can probably find it in Golden.

Golden Chamber of Commerce members rode the streetcar to Denver to advertise the reduction of round-trip carfare from seventy-eight cents to fifty cents. Standing left to right: Dr. Bill Peters, Harry Clift, Al Quaintance, O. A. Saunders, O. A. Nelson, Heinie Foss, John Q. Adams, Bill Fleming, Orville Dennis, Joe Kellogg. Front row left to right: J. Ed Dennis, George Hanel, Ted Grover. March 1941.

Chapter *Six*

Empire Builders: Business and Industry

The Rubey Bank building was constructed in 1873 by Louis J. Smith. Harry Rubey started as a clerk at the bank, working his way up to bank president.

The Rubey building is a wonderful example of the adaptive use of a structure. Today it houses a lingerie store and other businesses.

The spirit of free enterprise has always reigned supreme in Golden. As early as 1859, George West recognized the need for free commerce and competition. An excellent example of this was in pre-Prohibition Golden. Beginning in mid-1900, advertisements for Gustavus Schneller's Goosetown Tavern began appearing in the *Colorado Transcript*. The ad claimed his tavern was the only one in Golden selling Zang's Beer. "It makes your body strong and your heart glad!" was the catch phrase. Interestingly, Zang's was made in Denver. Goosetown was a Golden entity that owed its name to Adolph Coors' flock of geese running wild through the area north of Clear Creek. Needless to say, Schneller's ad and Coors' ad never ran on the same page in the *Colorado Transcript*.

Free enterprise came to a head in 2002 with the now famous "Coffee Wars." For years, only small, independent coffeehouses operated within the city limits of Golden, then suddenly, not one but two Starbucks franchises sprang up within two blocks of the downtown area. This caused quite a stir among Golden residents.

P. B. Cheney's Chicago Saloon opened its doors in 1861 and quickly became known as one of the most popular saloons in the Territory. While Golden was vying for the chance to be the territorial capital, Cheney supplied an abundance of ice and whisky to the legislators in the hope that the city would be chosen over Denver.

Chamber of Commerce

A longstanding complaint among Golden's business owners is that residents tend to shop outside of the community. In 1927, the *Colorado Transcript* ran the following admonishment:

> *We are living in a fast era. This is the day of the chain store; of the club and cooperative buying; the mail order houses...the automobile which so rapidly dissolves distance and makes it so easy for people to go elsewhere.*

The Golden Chamber of Commerce has been promoting the prosperity and welfare of the greater Golden trade area since its founding in 1920. Its mission has always been to help lure both businesses and shoppers back to Golden. The precursor to the Chamber was the Golden Commercial Club in the early 1900s. But the Club was not considered effective, and it disbanded. Today more than 525 members are committed to a healthy economy involved in competitive free enterprise and the coordination of profession, business, and industry.

Flour Mills

The rich soil of the Clear Creek valley made growing wheat a comparatively easy task. By 1866, Golden had two flour mills, the Star Mill and the Golden Mill.

The Golden Milling Company opened in 1867. The Peery family acquired the mill from Jesse Quaintance in 1900 and manufactured "Golden Seal Flour" until the mill closed in 1952.

Golden flour sack.

Star Mill

The Star Mill, also known as the Brick Mill, was founded in 1866 by William Lomax, Joel Palmer, and George Miller. The Star Flour Mill stood near the present-day location of 11th and Arapahoe Streets. The original Star Mill burned in August 1867, not an uncommon occurrence in those days. The structure was rebuilt and in production until 1888. The mill was eventually demolished, and nothing remains of it today.

Golden Mill

Founded in 1865, the Golden Milling Company began flour milling in 1867, near the present-day corners of Ford and 10th Streets, along Clear Creek's north bank. The mill was sold to Jesse Quaintance in 1876. The Golden Mill closed in 1898. In 1900, the mill was reopened as a combined operation with the nearby Binder Mill. When the Binder Mill burned in 1910, the Peery family acquired the Golden Mill and produced Golden Seal Flour until ceasing operations in 1952.

The modern-day incarnation of the Golden Milling Company is the Golden Mill Feed Store, located adjacent to the original location. The "new" building, constructed in 1923, utilized the original structure until 1952, when it was torn down. The parking lot marks the original location of the flour mill.

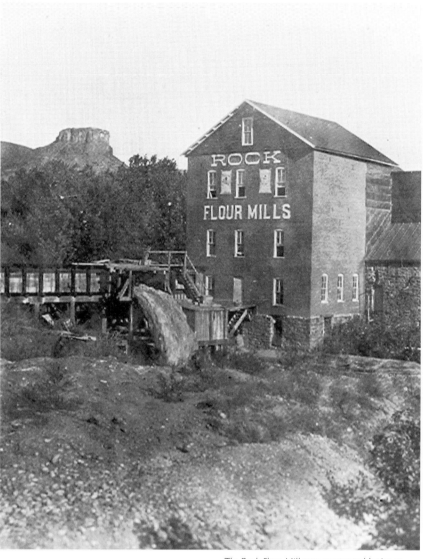

The Rock Flour Mill was constructed by Jonas and Oscar Barber in 1867. It closed briefly in 1880, when the stone burrs used for grinding the wheat became obsolete.

Barber's Rock Mill

The Rock Flour Mill was constructed by Jonas and Oscar Barber in 1867. It closed briefly in 1880, when the stone burrs used for grinding the wheat became obsolete.

In 1867, Jonas Barber raised the frame for a new flouring and saw mill in Golden—the Rock Mill, sometimes known as the Stone Mill. The Barbers' mill produced the "Shogo" brand of flour in the impressive edifice located between 8th and 9th Streets on Cheyenne Street. The mill was renovated in 1884 just prior to its sale to J.K. Mullen in 1885. By that time, the mill added a large warehouse. In 1899, John F. Vivian and J.K. Mullens formed a milling trust and paid five cents more per bushel of grain than their Denver competitors. Golden was attempting to corner the market on fine flour production. The mill ceased production and was decommissioned in 1965.

Today, parts of the Rock Mill are still visible on 8th and Cheyenne Streets in Golden. The large remnant warehouse structure houses a variety of businesses.

Binder Mill

The Binder Mill, founded in 1885 by Joachim Binder near 8th (now 18th Street) and Jackson Streets, was a relatively short-lived business in Golden. The mill was not powered by a water wheel mechanism, quite unique for the time. In 1898, it combined with the defunct Golden Milling Company. The mill burned to the ground in 1910.

Adolph Coors Industries

A Safe Substitute...

The international enterprise that is the modern Adolph Coors Industries had humble beginnings in Golden. The company's rise has been almost meteoric—from virtual oblivion to its current position as the third largest brewery in America as well as in industries seemingly distant from brewing one of America's favorite pilsners.

Early in 1867, Charles C. Welch and Henry Clements purchased a plot of land in eastern Golden to build a tannery. The tannery was in operation for several years before closing its doors and falling into some disrepair. Meanwhile, across the Atlantic Ocean in Hamburg, Germany, young Adolphus Herman Joseph Kuhrs was preparing to stow away on a ship bound for America.

Having served several apprenticeships at German breweries, the young stowaway had an idea of what he wanted to do in America. By 1872, Kuhrs had altered the spelling of his last name to Coors and arrived in Denver. There were, however, already seven breweries gracing the Queen City of the West, the largest being Philip Zang's brewery. Rather than trying to compete in the overburdened market, Coors purchased a stake in a Denver bottling works and began scouting potential brewery locations outside Denver. He settled on Golden because of its "can do" attitude, an available workforce, and an abundant water supply.

Coors partnered with Denver confectioner Jacob Scheuler in October 1873 to purchase the old Welch tannery and water rights for $2,500. They set out making major improvements to the site. But theirs was not the first brewery in Golden. That honor belonged to Bron and Koenig's

Coors Brewing Company ca. 1900.

Golden City Brewery. Undaunted, Coors intended The Golden Brewery to be the most extensive of its type in the Territory. He certainly had the expertise to brew a finer lager than most of the beer being brewed at the time.

Among the early equipment purchases were five twenty-barrel and twenty-five-barrel casks for fermenting, aging, and storing beer; a six-barrel mash tub; a ninety-barrel water tank; and various pumps, motors, and plumbing. By early February 1874, the ice house and ice pond were completed, and brewing commenced on February 27, 1874. The first barrel was ready for sale on April 1. The Golden Lager produced at Scheuler & Coors was a heavier beer with a more robust flavor than many of the beers of the time. It was an instant hit, necessitating expansion of the plant by the fall of that year, including a larger boiler room and pond. The lager was marketed as a "safe substitute for drink of a more ardent nature."

By 1878, the company added a bottling plant as well as a three-story 50-foot-by-50-foot malt house. By 1880, Scheuler & Coors ranked third among Denver-area breweries in production and sales with 3,004 barrels, behind Zang's at 8,408 barrels and the Denver Brewery at 5,858 barrels. That year, Coors bought out Scheuler's interest and commenced on a century of major growth. Interestingly, beer was more popular if served in bottles than on tap. It was presumed to be of a higher quality if the brewer invested in bottling the brew.

The Church and the Saloon...

In 1893, Coors' Golden Lager proved its worth when it competed against twenty-five other national beers at the Chicago World's Fair. It was the only brew made west of the Missouri River to receive an award for brilliancy, flavor, and chemical composition. But even this was not enough to keep the 19th Amendment from putting a stranglehold on the brewing industry. Colorado was under severe pressure from the temperance leagues to outlaw alcoholic beverages. Temperance slogans of the day included: "The Church and the Saloon both want your boy—which is going to get him?" The state passed a law on November 3, 1914, officially drying out the state on January 1, 1916. Coors watched as 17,391 gallons of his best were poured into Clear Creek on December 31, 1915. The nation followed suit with the 19th Amendment the following year.

Coors Brewing Company, 2003.

The master brewer was determined that the brewery would not close; Coors diversified his operation and put his son, Grover, in charge of the new "near-beer" and malted milk enterprises. The near-beer, dubbed Mannah and then renamed Coors Golden, was never a resounding success. When Adolph Sr. tasted the brew, he is said to have remarked, "It looks like beer, and it smells like beer, but it tastes like..." Eventually the process to create Mannah was refined, brewing a real beer, then distilling off the alcohol, which made a more palatable offering.

Malted milk proved to be more of a commercial success for the company than a financial one. The product was sold in various forms from powders to tablets to syrup. Coors' malted milk was of especially high quality because of its low moisture content. At a time when Coors most needed the support, Mars Candy Company came to the rescue, ordering as much malted

Coors Malted Milk advertisement. Courtesy Coors Brewing Company.

milk as Coors could produce. The product was an essential component of many popular Mars products. Coors ceased production of this product in 1957.

Brewers across the county were rapidly going under. Something had to be done. When Franklin Delano Roosevelt announced his candidacy for president, the brewers banded together and threw their collective support behind the man with the New Deal. One of Roosevelt's first acts was to push for the 21st Amendment, repealing Prohibition. At least in the beer market, happy days were here again. The Coors Brewery was one of the few breweries in Colorado to survive Prohibition, but sadly Adolph Coors, Sr., did not live to see the end of the law that almost cost him his brewery, having committed suicide in 1929.

The brewery was faced with hard times once again during World War II. Shortages of bottles, labels, tin cans, and gasoline often made production and shipping difficult. Overall, beer sales were down nationwide, as they were considered nonessential industries to the war effort. However, the government enabled the breweries to purchase wheat, barley and other essential ingredients provided the companies set aside 50 percent of their product for the men in uniform.

The Coors Mystique

After World War II, the brewery grew by leaps and bounds, leading the industry with innovations such as the recyclable aluminum can. In 1955, a Coors pilot plant began making aluminum beer cans. According to a plant spokesman, they had noticed the tin cans were being tossed along roadways and in fields, creating an unsightly mess, so by switching to aluminum, the plant could recycle the cans and reduce litter.

By the mid-1950s, Coors was producing a million barrels of beer annually—remarkable since Coors Beer was sold only west of the Mississippi River. It marked the beginning of the Coors mystique. People drove cross-country to take home cases of the brew; Presidents had it loaded onto Air Force One. It was a hit. The story line of the 1970s film "Smokey and the Bandit" centers on a trucker smuggling cases of Coors from Colorado to Atlanta. One other Colorado connection: the truck Burt Reynolds' character drives is from the Jolly Rancher Candy Company, another Colorado original.

The Coors Brewing Company continues to expand. The company assumed its place as the nation's third largest brewery in the 1990s. The distribution network went nationwide by the early 1990s. Coors became international by mid-decade. In 2002, the company invested in a brewery at Burton-on-Trent, England. Reality has far surpassed the vision of a man 130 years ago.

Coors Porcelain

Adolph Coors knew that diversification was crucial to his company. Man could not live by beer alone. In 1910, Coors teamed up with eastern pottery maker John Herold to open a porcelain plant at 8th and Ford Streets, the site of the old Coors, Binder & Company glassworks. During the middle of the decade, embargoes on German import porcelain created a market for high-quality scientific porcelains. Coors U.S.A. brand Thermo-Porcelain filled the niche. Adolph II and Herman, sons of Adolph, Sr., were placed in charge of the company.

Much of the early production was in dinnerware. The first lines were Glencoe and Thermo-Porcelain, then later, decalware and spongewear lines. Low-fire cooking and serving pieces came out in the mid-1930s with the popular Rosebud, Rock-Mount, Golden Rainbow, Golden Ivory, and Mello-Tone lines. The glaze and clay formulas for these lines have been lost, making the pieces highly collectible.

Production of home-use pieces ceased production in 1941 when Coors Porcelain reinvented itself as part of the U.S. war machine. The company provided porcelain housings for land mines and insulators. And according to the *Colorado Transcript*, the plant had an important role in producing the atomic bomb, which "brought about the immediate and unconditional surrender of the Japanese nation" (August 16, 1945). Coors Porcelain supplied the outer porcelain casings that held the bombs.

Coors Porcelain underwent a name change to CoorsTek. It continues to this day producing chemical porcelain for industry rather than home use. In 2002, the Coors family announced plans to regain control of the company. It has held 27 percent of the company for decades and intends to regain the remaining 67 percent of the stock. CoorsTek is a global company producing porcelain products for a range of uses and industries, among them: automotive, paper production, scientific labs, superconductors, aeronautics, and the U.S. defense industry.

June 1975
Coors brewery stock goes public

1978
Coors Light is reintroduced, becoming the "Silver Bullet" after a label redesign a few years later

1979
Herman Joseph's 1868, a more full-bodied beer, debuts

1982
Killian's Irish Red is introduced

1990
Coors purchases the Stroh's plant in Memphis, becoming America's third largest brewer

1991
Coors is finally available nationwide

1994
Coors sells 20 million barrels of beer in one year

1998
Coors celebrates 620 wholesale distributors worldwide

2002
Original Coors name changes to Coors Original

2003
Coors sells for $14.99 per case

Coors U.S.A. Chemical & Scientific Porcelain Company. During World Wars I and II, the company concentrated on the production of war-related products.

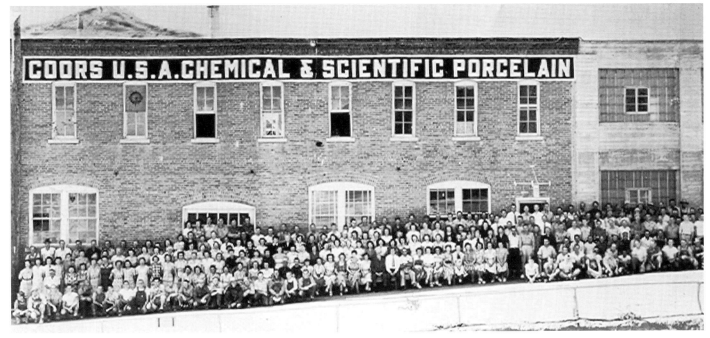

Foss General Store

In 1913, Henry J. Foss and his wife, Dorothy, purchased a Golden store front located on Washington Avenue and opened Foss Drug. It was only 1,200 square feet and was primarily a pharmacy. During Prohibition, pharmacies were permitted to sell alcohol for medicinal purposes. Foss, thinking ahead, acquired a liquor permit to dispense alcohol (the store retains the state's oldest permit, no. 1). When Henry Foss died, his son, Henry F., "Heinie," and widow, Dorothy, stepped in to run the business.

Prohibition was difficult for many businesses. To assist in keeping the Coors Brewing Company afloat, Foss began purchasing Coors' excess butter fat from the malted milk process, and Foss Perfection Ice Cream was born. This was soon followed by Foss Chocolates. Joe O'Byrne, Dorothy's second husband, purchased the Chocolate Shoppe in Golden to provide a suitable outlet for the ice cream and chocolate products. When O'Byrne died in 1929, Dorothy and Heinie sold the Chocolate Shoppe. In 1938, Heinie installed an ice cream freezer in the drug store so that ice cream could again be produced. In 1939, he expanded the store to the west, adding a soda fountain and luncheonette. That portion of the business, under Dorothy's careful tutelage, fared well until her death in 1963.

Foss continued to grow and diversify. The luncheonette became the 800-square-foot Golden Ram restaurant, located above the store. The restaurant closed in 2002 to make way for the Miner's Alley Playhouse and a yoga studio. The Foss store expanded its interests, leasing the old Everett Bank building on 12th Street and Washington Avenue for a clothing store—H. J. Foss Company. It closed in 2002, permitting more concentration on the renamed Foss General Store.

The Foss Drug Company opened its doors as a pharmacy and soda shop in 1913.

The Foss General Store proudly proclaims "Where the West Shops" on its storefront, 2003.

The store itself has had many renovations over the decades. For a while during the mid-twentieth century, it was a Walgreen pharmacy. Major renovations of the façade occurred in 1993 and again in 2003. In 1993, a mural by Robert Dafford was added to the south side of the façade, depicting some of Golden's notables, including Adolph Coors. The Foss General Store is truly an institution in Golden. Even with "big-box" competition, it retains its pharmacy status and, with that, its liquor license. In the spirit of its uniquely Golden heritage, Foss' motto is "Where the West Shops!"

Some of the many treats from the Jolly Rancher Candy Company.

Jolly Rancher Candy Company

Golden is traditionally known as the home of the world-renowned Coors Brewing Company. However, another world-famous treat had its origins in Golden as well. In 1949, Bill and Dorothy Harmsen chose Golden as the site on which to found their company, the Jolly Rancher. The company was a single storefront shop located on the east side of Washington Avenue at the base of the Welcome Arch, selling soft-serve ice cream and handmade chocolates. By 1951, Bill had created Fire Stix, a hard, cinnamon-flavored taffy with "intense" flavor. It was an instant success locally. The hard candy operation became so large that the factory was moved from Golden to the family farm in Wheat Ridge in the early 1950s. The ice cream and chocolate lines were gradually phased out until all Jolly Rancher made were hard taffies in a myriad of flavors.

The company was sold to Beatrice Foods in the 1960s, then to Hutamaki Oy in the 1980s. Hershey Foods Corporation purchased the factory in 1997. Jolly Rancher had gone international. In 2002, Hershey Foods made the decision to move Jolly Rancher production out of Colorado. The building that the original store had occupied for several decades is no longer there; it burned several times in the 1960s and was replaced by a larger brick structure.

Specialty Stores

Golden is small enough that it cannot hope to compete with the "big-box" stores and large malls that are within a few minutes, drive of the Golden city center. So, Golden business people have developed a unique collection of niche stores—specialty stores that cater to the visitor looking for that unique something. Its restaurants are also working to that end. These are just a few of the many stores and restaurants that contribute to Golden's historic character.

The Country Mouse, founded in 1983 as a framing and gift store, occupies a spot on Washington Avenue and carries many handmade items and Golden-specific gifts. Spirits in the Wind Gallery, also on Washington Avenue, features special shows and original works of art by noted Western and Southwestern artists. Meyer Hardware, founded in 1945 by Joe and Ruby Meyer, is a 38,000-square-foot small-town hardware store. Meyer's offers many things that the larger chain stores cannot provide, including exceptional customer service.

The Rock Rest started out in 1907 as part of the state rifle range at Camp George West. It was purchased during the 1920s by jazzman George Morrison and became one of the hottest jazz joints in the West. After serving its time as a bar and alleged brothel during World War II, the Rock Rest, located in Pleasant View, is now a popular barbecue joint and watering hole. The Old Capitol Grill, formerly Silverheels, occupies the hall constructed by William Loveland in 1863. The large brick edifice on 12th Street and Washington Avenue retains much of its character from the decades it spent serving as Golden's best-known department store, the Merc. Starbucks, a recent addition to the Golden scene, occupies the once proud and now revitalized Gem Theater building. The 13th Street Bakery inhabits a portion of Golden's imposing Armory Building, constructed in 1913.

The Everett building during restoration.

Fully restored, the Everett building now houses a clothing store, 2003.

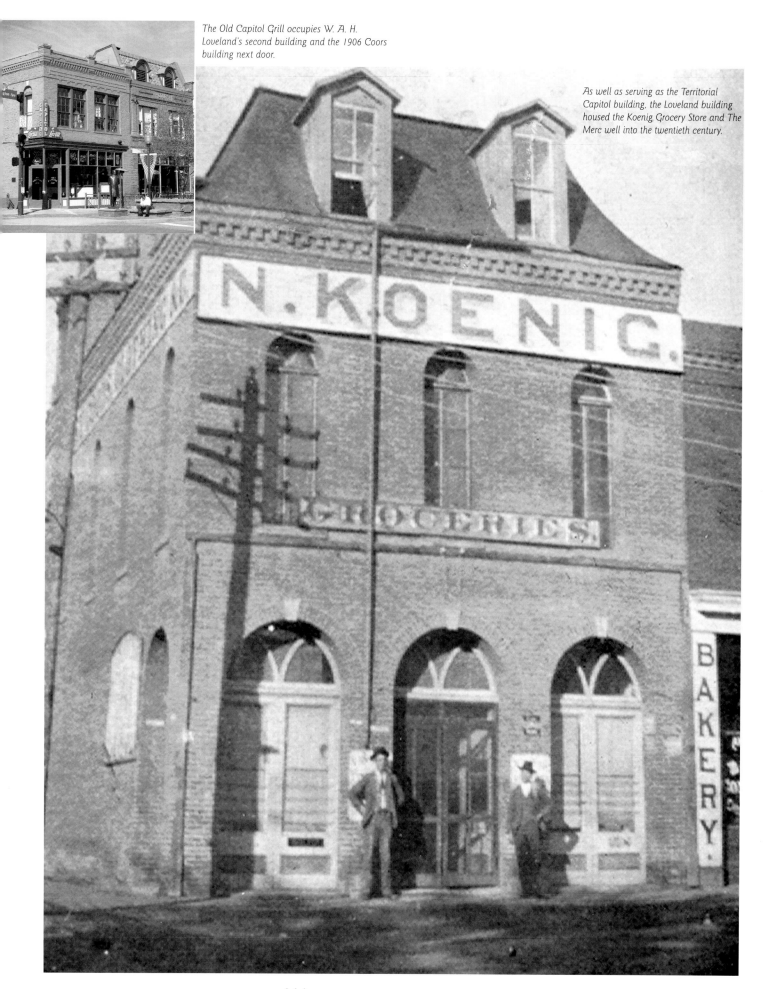

The Old Capitol Grill occupies W. A. H. Loveland's second building and the 1906 Coors building next door.

As well as serving as the Territorial Capitol building, the Loveland building housed the Koenig Grocery Store and The Merc well into the twentieth century.

N. KOENIG.

GROCERIES

BAKERY

Rocky Flats Nuclear Weapons Plant

Project Apple, a federal project whose mission was to locate a site for a new nuclear weapons plant, commenced in January 1951. The plant would produce plutonium triggers for atomic bombs. The list of possible sites was narrowed to nine over subsequent weeks: Amarillo, Texas; Oklahoma City, Oklahoma; Springfield, Missouri; Lincoln, Nebraska; Omaha, Nebraska; Topeka, Kansas; Colorado Springs, Colorado; Pueblo, Colorado; and Denver, Colorado. The Denver area seemed to be the ideal spot: it had a highly educated workforce, an airport, and a good climate. Seven sites were proposed within the area, three of which were in Jefferson County. A gently sloping plain just north of Golden received the final nod.

Rocky Flats, the local name for the area, was chosen because of the terrain—it was a combination of mesa and ravine, with a deep gravel bed for strong foundations. Water and electrical power were readily available, as was access to the Denver Rio Grande and Western Railroad and the new Moffat Tunnel. The land was inexpensive, and displacement of residents would be minimal. In addition, the climate's relatively calm winds were cited as a key deciding factor. This must have caused more than a few eyebrows to raise, considering the corridor between Golden and Boulder has long been known for extreme and dangerous windstorms.

On March 23, 1951, press conferences were held simultaneously in Denver, Los Alamos, and Washington, D.C., announcing the imminent construction of a new $45 million atomic energy plant. The announcement came as a surprise to Colorado Governor Dan Thornton, and Jefferson

The Rocky Flats site is a 6,380-acre Superfund cleanup site located eight miles north of downtown Golden. Until December 1989, the Rocky Flats plant produced components for nuclear weapons using various radioactive and hazardous materials, including plutonium, uranium and beryllium. Courtesy Department of Energy.

County, Boulder and Golden officials, as the Atomic Energy Commission had neglected to tell them of the impending construction. Overall, reaction was positive. Golden Mayor Everett Barnhardt said the plant would likely create a housing shortage in Golden but hoped that the result would be a better road to Boulder. Jefferson County assisted by banning all new construction until the plant was built so that available men and resources could be directed toward this new national defense endeavor.

Production began in fall 1952. The plant manufactured the plutonium pits or triggers for hydrogen bombs. It was one of several facilities constructed in the 1950s for the mass production of atomic weapons. Other plants included the Lawrence Livermore Lab, Sandia Labs, the Mound Plant, the Pantex Plant, and the Pirella Plant. Rocky Flats, as it was christened, had 100 permanent buildings and eighty trailers on its 384-acre site. Initially, 200 people were employed at the site. By 1992, that number had grown to 8,900, many involved in the decommissioning of the site. The last weapons-grade plutonium was shipped out of Colorado in June 2001.

Having the nation's largest producer of weapons-grade plutonium just eight miles from the center of town worried many residents. Efforts to comfort the populace had begun back in the 1940s after the drop of atomic bombs on Japan. The first "atomic town meeting" was held in Golden in January 1948. The thought was that the Table Mountains would shield the community from radioactive waves should an attack ever be launched on Denver. The efforts to comfort the community continued with an August 1955 forum where firefighters warned of the dangers of the nuclear age. Sergeant George Orsten, an instructor of radiological warfare at Lowry Air Force Base, indicated that the only way to avoid exposure was to evacuate should an accident or attack occur.

A Rocky Flats employee holds a plutonium button. The site's primary mission was to machine hockey-puck-sized pieces of plutonium, called "buttons," into hollow hemispheres. The last weapons-grade plutonium was shipped out of Colorado in June 2001. Courtesy Department of Energy.

Activities at Rocky Flats were suspended in 1989 after an FBI study found evidence of illegal dumping of toxic materials. Operations ceased in 1995; since then, the site has been in the process of a Superfund cleanup operation. Among the contaminants being cleaned from the 6,380-acre impact area are plutonium, uranium, and beryllium. The waste has been classified as containing alpha-emitting elements with an atomic number over that of uranium, having a half-life greater than twenty years and therefore hazardous, or transuranic. Much of the waste from the plant, including contaminated soils, asphalt, and gravel, are being sealed into transuranic waste containers (TRU-pacs) and transported to storage facilities in New Mexico and South Carolina.

When the site is clean, the area will become a national wildlife refuge.

NREL

In modern Golden, science is one of the primary industries. Leading the way is the National Renewable Energy Lab, or NREL. Established in 1974 by the Solar Energy Research Development and Demonstration Act, the Solar Energy Research Institute, as it was known initially, opened its doors in July 1977. Since 1991, NREL has been a national laboratory of the U.S. Department of Energy. The 300-acre campus is located on the southern flank of South Table Mountain. The mission of the lab is to develop renewable energy and energy-efficient technologies and practices, advance related science and engineering, and transfer knowledge and innovations to address the nation's energy and environmental goals.

Among the research programs that NREL is actively engaged in are basic energy research, photo-voltaics, wind energy, energy-efficient building technologies, advanced vehicle technologies, solar thermal electric, hydrogen, superconductivity, and geothermal power. To date, NREL's research has successfully and substantially lowered the overall costs of renewable energy generation. For example, wind power has gone from forty cents per kilowatt hour to less than five cents.

More than 1,000 people are employed at NREL, adding greatly to the economic viability of Golden. In addition, NREL's presence contributes to the national and international visibility of Golden in the sciences.

NEIC

Founded as part of the U.S. Geological Survey, the National Earthquake Education and Information Center is also located in Golden. The center, situated on the Colorado School of Mines campus, monitors earthquakes worldwide. Its mission, as part of the National Earthquake Hazards Reduction Program, is to provide and apply relevant earthquake science information and knowledge toward reducing deaths, injuries, and property damage.

Golden was founded as an entrepreneur's paradise. David Wall saw agricultural opportunities. George West envisioned a town of commerce. William Loveland beheld industry and government. Golden benefited from the visions of the founding fathers (and mothers). Business and industry came to Golden and has thrived. It is not only an economic center but an educational one as well. Golden also benefited from some dreams not coming to fruition. Loveland worked diligently toward making the town into the capital of the Territory and, ultimately, the State of Colorado. This venture failed, perhaps to Golden's advantage. The railroads and major highways, too, passed around rather than through Golden. This has enabled the town to remain quaint and quiet, fostering something that even the town fathers knew was imminent—tourism.

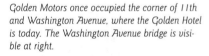

Golden Motors once occupied the corner of 11th and Washington Avenue, where the Golden Hotel is today. The Washington Avenue bridge is visible at right.

The dedication of the new Washington Avenue bridge completes a twenty-year project between the City of Golden and the Urban Drainage and Flood Control District. The bridge affords beautiful vistas of Clear Creek and the surrounding area.

Golden's first public school, 1866.

Chapter Seven

Scholarly Pursuits

While being used as a private residence, Golden's first public school structure suffered a fire in 1998. Fully refurbished, the building is a notable example of the adaptive use of a historic building.

Golden's status as a supply center and business town made it attractive to families. Men such as William Loveland brought their wives and children out to the frontier town very early in its history, creating a need for educational institutions. The first school was established in January 1861, with Thomas Dougherty providing instruction. Eighteen students had enrolled by January 11. It was a privately funded institution with all grades represented. By fall, a second teacher was added to accommodate the rapidly growing number of pupils.

Golden's first public school building was constructed in 1863 on 3rd Street (now 13th Street). The single-story brick structure served the needs of Golden's children until a new building was completed in 1867. The new structure, located on 5th Street (now 15th Street) and Washington Avenue, was not endowed with sufficient funds for seating, so benches were placed around the walls for the students to sit on. It opened in January 1867 with sixty-two students and two teachers, and it remained in use until 1873.

South School

By 1873, the little one-room school was filled to capacity, so work began on a new brick school at 3rd (now 13th Street) and Cheyenne Streets to relieve overcrowding at the small school on Washington Avenue. But from the beginning, South School, as it was called, was also overcrowded. The two-story edifice opened in October 1873 with forty-five students in the grammar grades, forty-eight in the intermediate grades, and seventy-nine in the primary grades. There were three teachers and a principal.

The South School was built in 1873 from commonly used soft brick and mortar.

Children were taught based on their age rather than on a "grade" division. By 1881, the school system was divided into ten grades. Jefferson County was the first district in the state to adopt this system. At South School, the lower grades were taught on the first floor, the upper grades on the second floor. By 1878, the number of students in Golden had doubled. Nearly all of them attended South School. The first graduating class held commencement exercises in June 1886 at the Golden Opera House, with eleven students receiving diplomas. By 1901, Golden's schools were considered among the best in the state, second only to Denver's East High School. And in May 1907, the youngest high school graduate in Golden gave the valedictory address. Carl Schoder was fifteen years old when he enjoyed that distinction.

South School was expanded over the years but could no longer meet the ever-growing demands of the modern educational system. It was sold to the Colorado School of Mines in 1936 to house the new geophysics department and was later converted to storage space. In 1965, the building was torn down.

North School

Prior to 1879, a small classroom in the Swedish Lutheran Church served the educational needs of many of Golden's north-side students. It was soon clear, though, that a building was needed to relieve the overcrowding of both the classroom and the South School. In fall 1879, construction began on a two-story brick structure at Payette Street (now 6th Street) and Washington Avenue. The school, dubbed North School, opened on March 6, 1880. That fall, students were divided by residence and age between North and South Schools. All Golden students above the sixth grade would go to South School. All students below the seventh grade would go to the school on the same side of the creek as their residence.

In 1937, North School was purchased by Jefferson County, and students were moved to the new Central School. The building housed the new Pioneer Museum and the Jefferson County Welfare Department. During World War II, the ration board could be found there. The building was demolished in 1965 to make way for Highway 58.

North School ca. 1910. By the mid-1960s, the building had fallen into dangerous disrepair and was demolished.

Before Central School was built, the site was occupied by the Bella Vista Hotel. Believing that Golden would need a first-rate hotel to serve the hoped-for Union Pacific Railroad traffic, the City Council asked citizens to contribute $5,000 toward the $50,000 cost of construction. The grand seventy-five-room hotel opened its doors on October 4, 1884, but the railroad never arrived, and the hotel was a failure. The structure was torn down in 1920.

Central School

As Golden's population grew, school overcrowding necessitated the construction of a new school. A combined elementary and junior high school was constructed in 1936. The Central School was located near the site of the old Bella Vista Hotel in downtown Golden. Bonds, a federal grant, and the WPA paid for construction. Additional funds came from the sale of South School to the Colorado School of Mines and from the Jefferson County school fund.

Central School ceased to house the junior high grades in 1956 when those grades were moved to the old high school building at 10th Street and Washington Avenue. Central School's name

was then changed to honor Roger Q. Mitchell, the superintendent of Golden's schools. Many residents of Golden fondly recall attending Mitchell Elementary.

School attendance continued to grow, and Mitchell reached capacity by the early 1990s. The Jefferson County School District listed it as one of the schools in line to be replaced. They projected that by the end of the decade, a school designed for 600 students would be housing more than 1,000. The Golden Urban Renewal Authority purchased the school in 1995, and construction began on a new Mitchell Elementary on Golden's north side. It opened in August 1997. The old Mitchell School was demolished when it was determined that renovating would be cost-prohibitive. The site has been redeveloped into a senior housing complex, an office building, and a parking structure, and future residences.

Built on a portion of the Mitchell Elementary (formerly Central School), this office building now houses several businesses

Junior High and High School

When South School became too crowded to accommodate the burgeoning student population, the call for a separate high school was issued. *The Colorado Transcript* reported: "The progressive people of Golden have registered their wish for the improvement by a 231–34 vote...Will Golden have a new high school? Tell all the world she will." The new school opened to students on March 6, 1924, at the corner of 10th Street and Washington Avenue. The facility boasted an auditorium and a gymnasium. It offered courses in theater, art, music, and foreign languages, although in 1918, Jefferson County dropped German from the curriculum in response to the war in Europe.

A mural painted by Santa Fe artist Gerald Cassidy graced Golden High School in 1927. "The Dawn of the West," funded by banker Jesse Rubey, was to be historical and inspirational. The mural remains on exhibit in the building. By the 1950s, it was again apparent that another Golden school had reached capacity. During breaks between classes, boys used the east hallway to go from class to class while girls used the west hallway. A new high school was built on 24th Street, and the building on 10th Street became the junior high school.

At that time, all the junior high students were moved from Mitchell School into the building on 10th Street. Several renovations occurred, including the addition of locker rooms, a storage area, and a new cafeteria. Additional renovations took place in the 1970s. The library doubled in size, carpet covered the tile floors, and temporary classrooms sprouted on the school grounds. Enrollment was at an all-time high during the 1960s and 1970s.

After being restored in 1998 at a cost of $4.26 million, the building became the home of the American Mountaineering Center. New additions to the building raised the total cost of the project to $7.5 million.

The Golden High School Spanish Club on a picnic to Genessee Park May 12, 1894. The group left at 7 a.m. and returned at 6 p.m., traveling in a wagonette pulled by four horses.

During the 1980s, the school's enrollment dropped off dramatically. The decrease in student numbers meant that the school had difficulty participating in intramural sports. To further the blow, the school district was converting most junior highs into middle schools and making high schools four years. The district would no longer sustain Golden Junior High School (GJHS). The school closed on May 7, 1988. Students were moved to Bell Middle School and Golden High School, depending on their grade level.

On March 6, 1924, the new Golden High School building opened its doors to much acclaim. The Class of 1956 was the last to graduate from the 10th Street and Washington Avenue school before it became the new home of Golden Junior High.

In 1992, the Golden Civic Foundation purchased the building for $50,000 and made it available to the American Alpine Club. The club, relocating from New York City, brought its extensive membership and 18,000-volume library with it. It invited the Colorado Mountain Club and its

Opened in 1956, the current Golden High School is again facing increasing enrollment challenges.

9,000-person membership roster to share the building. After extensive renovation and restoration, the two clubs moved into the old junior high. Colorado Outward Bound—an adventure-education organization serving primary and secondary school reform programs—soon joined them. Today, the building stands as a testament to adaptive use.

Bell Middle School, formerly Bell Junior High School, was built in 1963 to ease overcrowding at Golden Junior High School. Five hundred students were moved from GJHS to Bell when it opened. The school was designed to make use of the newest trend in education—"team teaching," in which classrooms could be opened up or subdivided by moving partitions. This enabled up to 120 students to be taught at one time in a single space. When Golden Junior High School closed, Bell took in the seventh- and eighth-grade students.

Golden High School lab students ca. 1900.

In 1986, the thirty-year-old Golden High School received a much-needed face lift. It had grown to five separate buildings that were combined into one facility. Today, Golden High School has approximately 1,350 students in grades nine through twelve. It is slated for yet another addition in the coming years. Its maroon and white mascot is the "Demon." Golden High is always a force to be reckoned with in athletics and academics.

Normal School

When people rushed west seeking a new life, many of them came without the benefit of a formal education. Still others, raised in rural areas, did not have access to schools during their childhood years. In the 1890s, Golden founded a normal school, geared toward educating these adults. The ninety-four students met at the South School. They took classes in physiography (geology and mineralogy), history, pedagogy, child studies, drawing, and physical culture exercises. Normal schools have evolved into the adult education classes given through the city and county recreation and extension offices of today.

Colorado State Industrial School

In January 1881, Governor Frederick Pitkin provided for the founding of a State Industrial School, a reform school for youthful offenders that would separate young boys from older criminals. Twenty-thousand dollars was to provide for its first two years of operation. The school would be situated on the grounds of the former Jarvis Hall and the newly vacated site of the School of Mines, to the south of Golden. Forty-two boys were housed there by December 1881.

By August 1881, the *Golden Globe* was boasting, "No Golden boy has yet been sent to reform school." The paper admonished that anyone witnessing boys gambling would do well to tell on them and get the boys sent to the school to learn good habits and not vices. Later that same year, the courts inadvertently remanded a young girl from a house of ill repute to the school, not knowing that it was designed to accommodate boys. The girl was apprenticed to one of the faculty members until alternate arrangements could be made for her.

Within one year, the school had reached capacity, so the State Legislature appropriated $60,000 for improvements and new construction on the site. By June 1882, 116 boys called the site home. The boys were educated in trade skills. Younger boys worked in the kitchens; older boys were trained in the tailor shop, gardens, orchards, animal barns, and carpentry shops. The school had its own shoe and broom shops. Surplus items were sold to the public, and the funds used to supplement the state's financial support. The school even had its own brick works. Charles Huscher, a faculty member of the school in 1900, advocated the work programs whose "aim is to teach the boy that labor is not a disgrace."

Much of the water supplying the school came from a spring on South Table Mountain and an on-site well. The abundant water and a land purchase of forty acres enabled the school to grow an abundance of alfalfa, beans, apples, pears, cherries, and plums. The boys raised all the produce needed for a year. In 1889, for example, the supply on hand for winter included five tons of beets, six tons of carrots, one and a half tons of turnips, four tons of parsnips, two tons of cabbage, three tons of onions, and two tons of squash.

Of the eighty boys housed at the State Industrial School in 1882, only four had any formal education, forty-three could not read, fifty-three could not write, and fifty had no understanding of mathematics.

Since the beginning of the twentieth century, the school has undergone several transformations. Emphasis has shifted away from mere punishment to building self-esteem and encouraging the residents to become productive members of society. Expanded and remodeled facilities assist in those endeavors. A new gymnasium was constructed in the 1960s, as were new living quarters. Additional residences were built in the 1980s, allowing each student to have a private room.

Today, the Lookout Mountain Youth Services Center, formerly the Industrial School, is a division of Colorado's Youth Corrections, one of several similar sites scattered throughout the state. At the center, young people who have been incarcerated for a variety of offenses receive counseling, complete their education through the GED program, and learn a variety of trades.

Colorado School of Mines

George West issued a call for a School of Mines in the July 21, 1869, issue of the *Colorado Transcript*:

The Hall of Engineering at the Colorado School of Mines was built in 1894 at a cost of $20,000; it is the oldest remaining building on campus.

> *The establishment at Golden City of a literary institution of high rank for boys, to be shortly developed into a University, is a matter of no small importance. The usual schools of Divinity, Law, and Medicine will doubtless soon be added, but the school in which the people of this and the adjoining Territories will feel the greatest interest is a School of Mines.*

This editorial was likely precipitated by a visit from the esteemed survey party of F. V. Hayden. The July 14, 1869, *Transcript* makes note that arrival of the party was imminent. Considerable space in the subsequent issue notes that the men camped on the ridge above the paper mill. Included in the party's ranks are a geologist (Hayden), a metallurgist, a botanist, and an ornithologist. Upon their departure, Hayden left a letter, dated July 22, 1869, that praised Golden, its geology, its abundant fire clays and coal, the prosperous farming, its energy, and the intelligence of the citizens. The banner for a Golden-based School of Mines followed rapidly on the heels of this momentous visit.

Hall of Engineering, Colorado School of Mines, 2003.

The first government appropriation of funds was in February 1870, when $3,872.45 was earmarked under the "Act to Establish a School of Mines." The money was to erect a brick building adjacent to the Episcopal institution Jarvis Hall. Instruction would be given in chemistry, mineralogy, metallurgy, and geology. Almost immediately, complaints arose about the school being placed under the auspices of the Episcopal Church. Indeed, Denver and Central City were among the most vocal in their opposition. The *Central City Daily Register* stated: "There is a point vastly deeper in this misappropriation than any ever hinted at by the (Colorado) *Transcript*. It is the bestowing of money belonging to the people of every religious faith on a sectarian college." Despite objection, the cornerstone was laid on August 8, 1870, on land donated by C. C. Welch. In 1872, the Territorial Legislature bowed to pressure, and under the Act of 1872, returned control from the Episcopal Church back to the Territory. However, it neglected to enforce the act, and church management of the School of Mines continued until 1874. The School of Mines opened for classes in 1873.

In 1874, Golden was faced with losing the School of Mines to Denver. Through the combined will of Charles Welch, William Loveland, George West, and Edward Berthoud, a legislative bill was passed in February 1874 that provided for the school's establishment as a territorial institution, located in Golden, Colorado, Territory. A Board of Trustees was appointed as well. According to the February 6, 1901 *Colorado Transcript*:

> *The territorial legislature of 1874 will be remembered in years to come by the fact that it established the State School of Mines of Colorado. It doesn't make any difference what else that the legislature may or may not have done or left undone. This one act is enough to redeem it from oblivion.*

The school boasted some of the most remarkable facilities for its time. There were four furnaces in the basement: one for an eight horsepower boiler, one for roasting ores, one for making assays, and another for "manufacturing." The laboratories were equipped with a geometer and reagent tables. An assaying office and weighing room as well as a mineral exhibition hall could be found in the building. Six faculty members, including Edward Berthoud and Arthur Lakes, guided the students through a curriculum of pure chemistry, applied chemistry, analytical chemistry, metallurgy, mineralogy, mining engineering, geology, and botany. In the early years, most of the students were interested only in a study course amounting to a few months about assaying. The school's name evolved from the Territorial School of Mines to the State School of Mines to the Colorado School of Mines.

Strong leadership helped to propel the school forward. Regis Chauvenet came in as president in 1883. By then, the Colorado School of Mines had moved from its original site in southeast Golden near the present-day Lookout Mountain School to its present site in the heart of Golden. Chauvenet had a vision for Mines far beyond the place it occupied. He began in earnest to apply the four-year engineering curriculum and to phase out the short-term assaying program. He also maintained strict adherence to keeping students in the coursework that they were academically prepared for rather than allowing students to flounder in courses for which they were not prepared. Under his guidance, the Chemistry Building and the Hall of Engineering were constructed. He also secured funding for an assay building, known as the Experimental Plant, and for Stratton Hall.

President Emeritus Dr. Melvin Coolbaugh acknowledged the stewardhip of Mines in 1949:

> *Mines was brought through its formative years by some of the truly great men of early Colorado. They did an enormous amount of work and planning for it, with little material reward.*

Berthoud Hall was named for Edward L. Berthoud, who was one of the original five faculty members at the State School of Mines.

Berthoud Hall, Colorado School of Mines, 2003.

In 1880, Mines had a student body of eighteen regular students and fifty-one "special" students, of which thirteen were women who attended lectures and drawing classes. The first woman to attend Mines as a regular student was Florence Caldwell Jones. Having received her bachelor's degree from Ohio Wesleyan University in 1890, Caldwell entered Mines in 1895 as a sophomore and graduated three years later with a degree in civil engineering. The first women's residence at Mines was named for her.

Many more women would follow. Grace McDermut's family owned a gold mine, and planning for her future in the family business, she became a member of the 350-man freshman class in 1899. She was the only female. McDermut graduated with an engineer of mines degree in 1903 and became the first woman hired by the National Bureau of Standards. Women in the early years at Mines remember a lack of ladies' restrooms; in addition, they weren't allowed in the men's dining halls and had to dine off-campus.

Over the decades, the presence of women on campus has grown steadily. In 1964, the first women's residence was opened at the former Dean of Students' house. In 1968, the first residence hall for women opened. In 1975, the first sorority house—the Alpha Delta— opened, and in the 1980s Mines graduated its first female Ph.D. candidate—Ramona Gonzalez, who received the honors in petroleum engineering. In 1998, Mines graduated its 2,000th female student. Today, women comprise about 25 percent to 30 percent of the student population.

Other than the red-roofed buildings dotting the western edge of downtown Golden, the most visible sign of Mines is the prominent "M" on the side of Mount Zion. While visitors to Golden often puzzle over its meaning—Morrison, mountain, what?—it has always stood for the school's erstwhile moniker, simply "Mines." The idea was based on a "U" gracing the campus

The School of Mines Freshman Class, 1895.

To many, the Colorado School of Mines' "M" not only proclaims the proud heritage of the university, but also the unique and significant contributions of the Golden community to Colorado.

above the University of Utah. Installation took place in 1908. The 104-foot-by-107-foot M-blem is composed of white-washed stones, each weighing roughly six pounds. It has long been the manifestation of the rivalry existing between Mines, the University of Denver (DU), and the University of Colorado (CU). In 1919, DU students were caught trying to paint it red; their heads were shaved and painted with a silver nitrate "M." While not permanent, the not-so-subtle reminder served as a warning to others who might attempt sabotage against a school with some very novel methods of retaliation. Each fall, the freshman students gather stones and climb the mountain to repair and whitewash the M. Each spring, the seniors repeat the rite.

In 1932, the "M" was electrified. It had, on occasion, been lit for special events. "Cement" Bill Williams helped set the poles for the lighting. Periodically, throughout the year, the students will change the lighting to reflect particular things. For example, at the end of the school year, the lights change to reflect the number of days left in the school session. During the holidays, the lights are often red or green. And as a show of patriotism, they have been changed to a progression of red, white, and blue from south to north.

The Colorado School of Mines is recognized worldwide for its progressive approach in educating the world's future engineers. In 1907, it became the first mining school in the United States to purchase a mine for educational purposes. The mine, located on Mount Zion, was equipped with electricity and a blacksmith's shop. Today, Mines uses the Edgar Mine in Idaho Springs to teach students and to provide a real environment in which they can test the ideas and technology constantly under development on campus. An Experimental Plant, later called the Research Institute, was constructed in 1911 along the south side of Clear Creek for the testing, treatment, and extraction of ores. The plant has since been dismantled.

In 1949, a prediction was made that when the first manned expedition landed on the moon, the astronauts would look out the windows and see a figure in a patched space suit chipping away with a rock hammer, and stenciled on the suit would be the words, "Property of the Colorado School of Mines, USA, Earth." While that did not come to pass, the school remains at the cutting edge of technology in a multitude of areas. On the final mission of the space shuttle Columbia in January 2003, Mines students had placed onboard an experiment to test fire-suppression devices designed for use in space. The experiment was a success. Today, Mines is leading the way in biodetection of chemical and biological weapons. Researchers are working with others at Teledyne, Orbital Scientific, and other companies to develop technologies that can provide a chemical breakdown of a sample in about four minutes, determining if the sample contains bacteria, viruses, or chemical agents harmful to humans. The units are designed to be a mobile lab, mounted on a truck or military Humvee.

The Colorado School of Mines remains at the top of the academic pinnacle. It is one of the most respected mining and engineering schools in the world. Students from countries around the world seek out the college for its active research programs and world-class faculty.

George and Eliza West are seated bottom center, and standing to the right of George's shoulder is his son, Harl. Standing back center in white is Harl's wife, Vera Parshall West.

Chapter Eight

Faces of Golden

Women of the Goetze family.

Since its humble beginnings in 1859, Golden's impact on the world stage has been significant. Were it not for many devoted and determined people, the town would not have survived into the twenty-first century. Some of the people merely passed through on their way to bigger and better things, but others lived out their lives here, pursuing their dreams and ambitions. From railroads to Buckingham Palace, these are just a few of the people who gave Golden such an interesting past and a place in history.

Give 'em Hell, West

George West

It is quite possible that without two unique New Englanders, Golden would have faded into oblivion like so many other towns that sprang up during the early years of the Pikes Peak gold rush. One was the incomparable George "Give 'em Hell" West.

Born on November 6, 1826, in Claremont, New Hampshire, West had an enterprising spirit from an early age. At age fourteen, he apprenticed as a printer's devil on the *National Eagle* (Massachusetts) newspaper for three years. Following a stint with the *Boston Cultivator*, West began writing features for the *Boston Transcript*, a career move that would forever shape his life. During this period, West became involved with Company H of the 1st Massachusetts Volunteer Militia, ultimately being promoted to captain.

George West and son, Harley "Harl" West, and grandson, Neil West Kimball ca. 1899.

Word of gold discoveries at Pikes Peak began to filter to Boston in 1859. Like many of his contemporaries, West could not resist the glitter of both adventure and possible riches. In March 1859, the thirty-two-year-old and several friends formed the Mechanics Mining and Trading Company and hit the trail for the gold fields. He captained the wagon train that arrived in Denver City on June 10, 1859, after a journey of more than nine weeks. His first job was running the presses for fledgling newspaperman William Byers at the *Rocky Mountain News* for a story confirming gold strikes by John Gregory and George Jackson on Clear Creek.

West and his party, now called the Boston Company, continued on until they found a small settlement on the banks of Clear Creek. He was confident this would be the best spot to profit from the mining traffic. The Golden Town Company was formed on June 20, 1859, with West as president. His enterprises in Golden included starting the *Western Mountaineer* newspaper in 1859 and an express freight line to Denver City in 1861.

When the governor called for the formation of a volunteer militia to protect the Territory, West joined and became the captain of Company H in the Second Colorado Volunteer Infantry, which eventually became the Second Colorado Cavalry. His was the only Colorado unit to capture a

Confederate battle flag during the Civil War. During the war, West married Eliza Boyd, the daughter of one of Golden's founding families. The couple had five children.

Following the Civil War, West returned to Golden and in 1866 started his second newspaper, the *Colorado Transcript.* George and Eliza wrote for the paper. It remained in the family until 1960. West remained active in the militia, serving as the 13th adjutant general in 1887. He gained his nickname during this period when a conflict with the Utes broke out at Milk Creek and West signed a missive to Brigadier General Frank Reardon with "Give 'em Hell, West."

Known as a charming, gracious man, West was quite a character. Local legend has it that he was nearly drawn into two duels. Prior to the Civil War, Confederate sympathizer Dock Turpin rode through the street, loudly cursing Yankees. West chastised him through the *Western Mountaineer,* and as any self-respecting Southern man would, Turpin called West out. West chose the weapons and location: Bowie knives, with West standing on North Table Mountain, Turpin on South Table Mountain. The knives would be thrown a distance of half a mile. But the duel never took place, *and the two settled their differences over a glass of Cherry Bounce.* The second duel was with the editor of the *Golden Globe* over the alleged inappropriate purchase of a saddle horse with state funds. West's response to the challenge was, "Thundermugs at twenty yards, roll 'em or throw 'em." This time, the duel was averted over "a bottle of the best."

George West died on November 15, 1906, at age eighty. He is buried in the Golden Cemetery.

The Venture Capitalist

William Austin Hamilton Loveland

Golden owes a great deal to William A. H. Loveland, an enterprising New Englander whose name is known to many, though few know much about the man. In Colorado, a town, a mountain pass, and a mountain all bear his name.

Loveland, son of a Methodist preacher, was born in Chatham, Barnstable County, Massachusetts, on May 30, 1826. The family moved around a great deal, settling in Rhode Island before moving on to Brighton, Illinois. He was educated at McKendree College in Lebanon, Illinois, and Shurleff College in Upper Alton, Illinois. Loveland left college to join the army and fight in the Mexican War. While serving as the wagon master under General Winfield Scott Stratton in Mexico, he was wounded in the leg from an exploding artillery shell.

William A. H. Loveland.

Following his return from Mexico, Loveland caught the gold fever that was sweeping the nation. He set out in 1849 for the gold fields of California but was unsuccessful in his quest. He returned home to marry Philena Shaw. She died in 1854. Following a brief sojourn in Nicaragua, Loveland returned to Illinois to marry Miranda Ann Montgomery on August 25, 1856. He operated a mercantile for several years before succumbing again to the lure of the gold fields.

He arrived in Golden City on June 22, 1859, and immediately set out building a mercantile. He brought his wife and two sons to Golden in 1860. Loveland became active immediately in town politics and is listed as one of Golden City's founders. In April 1860, he became Golden's treasurer. It was his vision that Golden become the capital of the blossoming Colorado Territory. When the capital was moved from Camp Creek to Golden City, the Legislature met in the second floor of Loveland's mercantile building.

The Loveland Hose Company building now serves the American Legion Post and is one of only three buildings left standing in Golden that were built by Mr. Loveland.

The Golden Fire Department ca. 1920 stands in front of the Loveland Hose Company. From left, second row: Elmer Rowe, Bill Weber, Bill Rowe, Marvin Van Winkle, Tom Grenfell. Front row, from left: William Owens, Bud Lowe, Bill Arney, Jack Nixon, Adolph Coors Jr., Joe Coors, Russ Johnson, Ed Warren, George McCoy, Bill Volz, Bill Pomeroy, Doc Crawford.

Education was also of paramount importance to Loveland. He served on the Board of Trustees for the founding of the Denver Seminary—eventually the University of Denver. When the State School of Mines was founded, Loveland served in several capacities, including professor in charge and president of the Board of Trustees.

One of Loveland's greatest contributions to Colorado was his commitment to bringing railroads to the Territory. He commissioned Edward Berthoud to survey a route through the mountains with the intent of bringing the transcontinental railroad through Golden. While that did not happen, his Colorado Central Railway was a success, bringing ore from the mining towns and linking up with spurs to Denver and Longmont.

Politics continued to play a vital role in Loveland's life. He purchased the *Rocky Mountain News* in 1878 to use as a platform to run for governor but lost the election by a margin of only 3,000 votes. He served on the county commissions of Jefferson, Gilpin, Boulder, Clear Creek, and Larimer Counties. Various Boards of Directors also counted him on their rolls, among them mines and a pottery works.

Loveland died on December 17, 1894, at the age of sixty-eight. His wife passed away in August 1923. They are buried in Denver.

A Renaissance Man

Edward L. Berthoud

Many people have heard the name Berthoud. It graces a mountain pass, a town, and a building on the Colorado School of Mines campus, but few know anything of the man for whom they were named. Edward Louis Berthoud was born in 1828 in Geneva, Switzerland. When he was two, the family immigrated to New York, and he grew up in the Mohawk River Valley. Berthoud was not an especially gregarious man but possessed an indefatigable desire for knowledge.

Like his brother Alexander, Edward attended Union College and made such interesting friends as Chester A. Arthur and Frederick Seward. Berthoud graduated with a B.A. in engineering and worked on the Morris Canal and for the Panama Railroad Company. Following a year in the tropics, Berthoud began working his way westward with America's burgeoning railroad industry. He settled briefly in Logansport, Indiana, where he met his future wife, Helen Samaria Ferrell. They married in 1856.

In 1859, Helen's parents headed for the Colorado gold fields, and there is some discrepancy as to when the Berthouds followed. Some records indicate Berthoud was a Golden City founder, placing them in town by June 1859, but other records indicate they came west in March 1860. College associate Silas Burt joined him in May 1860, and the two set out surveying routes to

Edward Berthoud, noted geologist and surveyor.

the gold regions and the mineral deposits of the area. But Burt tired of the frontier life and returned to the East in October 1860.

When the Civil War broke out, Berthoud joined Company H of the Second Colorado Volunteer Infantry, serving under Captain George West. He worked as a local recruiter and as a field agent, finally transferring near the front, where he served as an adjutant for General Thomas Ewing at Kansas City. Berthoud never saw combat, but while serving under General James Ford, he engineered earthworks that sheltered the Union forces during battles with Confederate General Sterling Price's forces.

The "ghost" of Edward Berthoud appears each year for the Golden Cemetery Tours. In 2002, he was seen chatting with another "ghostly" fellow, Golden entrepreneur Charlie Quaintance.

The Berthouds returned to Golden in 1866, and Edward was elected to the Territorial Legislature on the "Unionist" Radical Republican ticket and was chosen Speaker of the House. To the dismay of fellow Republicans, Berthoud was really a Democrat. He never again sought public office, though he held many appointed posts including territorial treasurer and territorial librarian.

Berthoud is best known for his survey work, at which he excelled. He kept extraordinarily busy. Among his numerous projects: Berthoud Pass, the Colorado Central Railway, the Golden and South Platte Railway & Telegraph, a rail line from Cheyenne to the Black Hills, the Georgetown Loop, the Vasquez Flume & Ditch, the Golden Ditch & Flume, and the Denver, Lakewood & Golden interurban line.

But surveying and designing railways were not his only interests. Berthoud took copious notes, wrote articles on birds and trees, Native American rock art, underground water resources, and the French exploration of the American West. He published a book on the Ice Age and Pliocene Man, an article in *National Geographic* on Sir Francis Drake's anchorage in California, and a treatise on the Natchez Indians. His eclecticism served him well as one of the founders of and early instructors at the State School of Mines.

Helen Berthoud died from a stroke on July 29, 1887, and Edward wrote of her passing: "Loved forever, we hope to meet again." Berthoud continued working for the remainder of his life, and many unfinished projects were found in his effects. Early in 1908, he began to suffer from dizzy spells and collapsed and died probably from a stroke on June 13, 1908. Berthoud, who had a lifelong fear of being buried alive, had requested that his body be held for an extra day before burial in the Golden Cemetery.

A Western Lady

Louise Caroline Millikin

Louise Caroline Chalfant was born in 1836 in Waynesburg, Pennsylvania. At age nineteen, she married Robert Millikin, a carpenter from a neighboring township. Their first child, James Madison, was born a year later.

In 1857, Robert and his father caught "westward fever." Both families sold their homes, loaded their belongings into ox-drawn wagons and started west. It was a grueling trip through Ohio, Indiana, Illinois, and then crossing the Mississippi River into Hannibal, Missouri. The party arrived in Lincoln, Nebraska, and decided to apply for a homesteads in Rock Bluff. They received their homesteads in August. After purchasing cattle and supplies, they made the three-day journey to Rock Bluff. By October, they had built fences and a five-room house that Robert and Caroline shared with his parents.

In July 1858, Caroline gave birth to their daughter, Lydia, named for Robert's mother. At the time, Robert was working as the town contractor. He had to build a new house for their growing family when Caroline gave birth to son William. They welcomed son Francis in 1862. In 1863, son Lee was born, named for Robert's lifelong friend, Lee Harsh. In 1869, daughter Minnie was born, and in 1871 came son Robert Jr. Florence followed in 1874 and John in 1876, but he died six months later of "crib death."

When gold was discovered in the western Kansas Territory, Robert was ready to head farther west. The Millkins sold their homestead, packed their belongings, and headed for Black Hawk. There Robert filed a mining claim and built a small house. Caroline met Augusta Tabor, and the two became lifelong friends.

But tragedy arrived with the family. In July 1860, their son James fell into the mineshaft and drowned. Financially, the family did well in the mines; both Robert and Caroline held claims. Robert worked as a cabinetmaker to supplement the family income. But, for all their success, tragedy continued to haunt them. In 1865, typhoid hit Black Hawk, taking both William and Lee. Lydia contracted it and was severely weakened but survived another eight years. In 1866, daughter Ida was born; she died less than a year later.

The great-granddaughter of Caroline Millikin, Cynthia Jennings, portrays her ancestress during the 2003 Golden Cemetery Tours.

Robert and Caroline sold their claims in 1867 and moved to Golden City, where Robert founded Millikin and Lee Construction. His firm constructed the first Jefferson County courthouse. In addition to construction, Robert was elected to serve as Golden's mayor in 1872 and as a County Commissioner in 1879. Robert died of pneumonia in March 1884.

Caroline was left with the construction business and four surviving children. She sold the company and became a midwife to support her family. She once said, "After ten children, who would be more qualified than I?" Caroline died December 1923 at age eighty-seven. Both she and her husband are buried in the Golden Cemetery.

Astor House Matron

Ida Goetze

Ida Goetze was born in Lobenstein, Germany, in 1854. At age twenty, she immigrated to the United States, settling in Terre Haute, Indiana. In 1880, she returned to Germany for a year but came back to Terre Haute. In 1883, she moved to Denver, where she met Henry Goetze, a Civil War Union veteran, whom she married in 1885.

The Goetzes moved to the mountain enclave of Georgetown, Colorado, where sons George and Oscar were born. In 1891, Henry died, and Ida moved her household to Golden. Mrs. Goetze could not speak English at that time, so she studied in the evenings with her sons to learn the language.

To support her family, Mrs. Goetze purchased the Astor House at 12th and Arapahoe Streets, made improvements to the building, and ran a boardinghouse. She sold it when she was in her seventies. Always civic-minded, Mrs. Goetze was a member of the T. H. Dodd GAR Post, and the Relief Corps.

Following a fall, Mrs. Goetze's health began to decline. She died in February 1936 at the age of eighty-two. She was survived by her son, Oscar.

Ida Goetze and sons, Oscar and George, ca. 1895.

Goetze family ca. 1965.

Larger than Life

William F. Cody

Among Golden's many memorable characters stands the seemingly larger-than-life specter of William F. "Buffalo Bill" Cody—America's most flamboyant showman and western ambassador. Cody's connections to Golden in life were slight. The great showman is buried atop Lookout Mountain, forever gazing over the little town that reveres its connection to the man.

Cody was born in 1846 in Le Clair, Iowa, to Isaac and Mary Ann Cody. When young Bill was seven, his father moved the family to Kansas Territory and became a trader, working with the Indians in the area. At age thirteen, Bill left home for the Pikes Peak gold fields. Dissatisfied with the prospects in Denver City, he signed on with the fledgling Pony Express Company and became one of its youngest and most famous riders. Cody once rode 322 miles in twenty-one hours and forty minutes, wearing out some twenty horses in the process.

His speed and prowess on horseback were attractive to the Union Army, which hired him from 1861 to 1863 to carry dispatches in Kansas, Missouri, and along the Santa Fe Trail. After the death of his mother, Cody joined the Kansas Volunteer Infantry.

After the Civil War, Cody held a various jobs, including stage driver. His most dangerous encounter occurred in March 1866 when he married Louise "Lulu" Frederici of St. Louis. He and Lulu would always have a contentious relationship, and she eventually sued (unsuccessfully) him for divorce in the years just prior to Cody's death. Lulu blamed their troubles on his predilection for women and alcohol. Cody blamed it on her tendency to consult psychics about their marriage. The couple had three daughters and one son. Only one daughter survived her parents.

Cody earned his nickname, "Buffalo Bill," while he worked for the Kansas Pacific Railroad as a buffalo hunter in 1867–68. It is recorded that he shot 4,280 buffalo in his eighteen-month employment. Cody moved on to become a government scout at Fort Larned, Kansas, and then with the 5th Cavalry 1868–72. He was elected to the Nebraska Legislature on the Democratic ticket but left in 1873 to pursue other interests.

"Buffalo Bill's Wild West" was organized in 1883. It was one of the most spectacular of the Wild West shows touring the United States at that time. Cody's show featured women sharpshooters, Indian battles, and hundreds of animals. The show toured Europe twice and went broke with extreme regularity. He became one of the charter members of the Showmen of America.

In 1896, Cody founded the town of Cody, Wyoming.

After the lights went down on the Wild West, Cody began to slip further into the alcoholism that had plagued him for years. He died at his sister's home in Denver on January 10, 1917. Cowgirl Goldie Griffith recalled that Cody took her to the top of Lookout Mountain and pointed out the amazing view, indicating that he wanted to be buried on the spot just above Wildcat Point. The people of Colorado obliged and blasted a burial site from the rock on the mountain. He was laid to rest on June 3, 1917, with full Masonic burial rites performed by George W. Parfet, Worthy Master of Golden City Lodge Number 1. More than 20,000 paid their respects to the man who brought the essence of the Wild West to the world.

William F. Cody ca. 1890. Buffalo Bill Cody was known for his excellent treatment of all who worked for him, paying everyone equal wages.

Coors family photo ca. 1890.

A Rocky Mountain Legend

Adolph Coors

Many of America's success stories arise from the trials and triumphs of immigrants who came seeking a better life, a second chance, an opportunity. The story of Adolph Coors is just such a tale.

Adolphus Kuhrs was born on February 7, 1847, to Joseph and Helena in Westphalia, Germany. The family was Prussian of Dutch descent. His father moved the family several times seeking work. At age thirteen, Adolph was apprenticed at Andrea and Company and learned the printing trade over the next nineteen months. The family moved again, and Adolph hired on as an apprentice to the braumeister at the Henry Wenkler brewery, one of the oldest in Germany. Apprentices were not paid, so he earned money as a bookkeeper for the brewery. He stayed there until 1867 before moving on to breweries in other cities.

The men of the Coors family ca. 1990. Courtesy Coors Brewing Company.

In 1868, Adolph was of age to serve in the Prussian army. Rather than enter the compulsory service, the young man chose to stow away on a ship bound for America. He was soon discovered. Reaching port in Baltimore, Adolph worked off the cost of his passage as a bricklayer, stonecutter, fireman, and general laborer.

Working his way West, he arrived in Denver in 1872. At the time, there were already seven breweries in Denver. Seeing an opportunity, Coors (as he now chose to spell his name) bought an interest in a local bottling plant. On his day off, he would scout locations for a brewery of his own. He liked the looks of Golden. It had a booster spirit and a good water supply.

In October 1873, he partnered with local confectioner Jacob Scheuler to purchase the old C. C. Welch tannery on the eastern edge of Golden. Scheuler fronted $18,000 for the business, Coors only $2,000, but he had the expertise to brew fine golden lagers. The brewery grew by leaps and bounds. By 1880, it was the third largest beer producer in the Denver area.

Taking time away from his business was a rare occurrence for Adolph Coors. But in April 1879, he found the time to marry Louise Weber, the daughter of a local railroad superintendent. The couple built a beautiful home on the site of the Golden Grove Pavilion. Together they had eight children; six survived into adulthood. Adolph would be able to pass the brewery safely into the hands of his three sons.

On January 1, 1916, the State of Colorado went "dry," and Coors was forced to pour 17,391 gallons of the golden lager into Clear Creek. Prohibition was a blow to the company and the man. Coors was determined that the operation would survive, and he developed creative methods for ensuring this outcome. Diversification was the key. The company manufactured porcelain, bottles, malted milk, and near beer. Adolph Coors died on June 5, 1929, without seeing the end of Prohibition and his company's return to the top of the American beer market. Adolph and Louise are buried near Golden.

A Spend-Nothing Governor

John C. Vivian

Born into a politically powerful family, John Charles Vivian's future was almost predestined. Vivian's grandparents were some of Arvada, Colorado's, early pioneers, having arrived in 1860. John's father, John F., became a chairman of the Jefferson County Republican Party. John Charles came along on June 30, 1889.

John graduated from Golden High School in 1905 and went on to the University of Colorado at Boulder. He was a bass drum player in the university's marching band. Following the completion of his bachelor of arts degree in 1909, Vivian went on to the University of Denver, completing a law

John C. Vivian as a paperboy ca. 1900.

Governor John C. Vivian served the state of Colorado for two terms during the 1940s.

degree in 1913. During his school years, Vivian was an avid writer, penning both poetry and prose. He worked briefly for both the *Denver Times* and the *Rocky Mountain News* before pursuing law full time.

Politics was endemic to the Vivian family, and John Charles was appointed Golden City attorney in 1914. Following a stint with the Marines in World War I, he returned to Golden and became Jefferson County attorney 1922–32. In 1939, he was chosen lieutenant governor in Ralph Carr's administration. The Republican Party chose him as its gubernatorial candidate in 1943.

Always a fiscal conservative, Vivian's governorship was a true hallmark of this trait. Rather than living in the Governor's Mansion, he lived at his home in Wide Acres in Golden and drove himself to work or took the streetcar. During his administration, no new taxes were enacted, official stationery was reused, and the number of state employees was reduced. Among his chief concerns were veteran's affairs, conservation, and highway safety. When he left office, there was a $13 million budget surplus in the Colorado State General Fund.

Having served two terms as Colorado's governor, Vivian made an unsuccessful bid for the U.S. Senate in 1948. He retired from public life and worked with the law firm of Vivian, Sherman, and Kinney. Vivian died on February 10, 1964, at age seventy-six and was interred in the Golden Cemetery.

George Morrison with his sister, Marian, his wife, Willa May, and aunt, Hattie McDaniels, Los Angeles, 1948.

Mr. Music

George Morrison

Denver's preeminent jazz musician, George Morrison, left a lasting impression on the town although he wasn't raised in Golden.

Born in Fayette, Missouri, on September 9, 1891, Morrison was destined for a life surrounded by music. Both parents were highly skilled musicians; his father was a fiddler, his mother a pianist. The family moved to Boulder, Colorado in 1900, bringing with them the family business, the Morrison Brothers String Band. No one in the family could read music; all played by ear. They were widely known for their upbeat renditions of popular tunes such as "Silver Threads among the Gold" and "After the Ball."

Morrison worked at the University of Colorado's Delta Tau Delta house as a cook to earn enough money to purchase a violin and saved enough money to take lessons from Howard Reynolds. He tried to join the Denver Symphony Orchestra, but was barred because he was black. Instead, Morrison played at Mattie Silk's House of Mirrors, the famed Denver parlor house. In 1911, Morrison married Willa May and moved to Denver.

In 1920, following a brief trip to Chicago, Morrison founded his first big band, which included Eugene Montgomery on drums, Jesse Andrew on piano, Ed Carwell on trombone, Ed Kelly on saxophone, Lee Morrison on banjo, Emilio Gargas on string bass, Cuthbert Byrd on saxophone, Lee Davis on trumpet, and Morrison on violin. The band played jazz, the latest and most controversial music of the time. Columbia Records soon invited them to cut an album.

"Cement Bill" Williams.

Golden came into Morrison's life in 1923 when he and a partner opened the Rock Rest club along the Denver-to-Golden road on the streetcar line. But it became a target for the local Ku Klux Klan, and Morrison sold it to tour with his band. Morrison hired an aspiring young singer and actress, Hattie McDaniel, for his vocal section, and the group toured the vaudeville circuit for many years. Morrison's band even played a command performance at Buckingham Palace for the crowned heads of England.

Morrison is best known for revolutionizing jazz by introducing the saxophone, and Golden was witness to it first. He also founded Musicians Local No. 623 union. In 1942, *Downbeat* magazine named Morrison the "Best Musician West of Kaysee" (Kansas City). Mr. Music, George Morrison, died in Denver in 1974.

Have Cement, Will Travel

William "Cement Bill" Williams

Every town has a memorable character best known for some unusual trait, hobby, or profession. In Golden's case, the character is William "Cement Bill" Williams. Born in East Orange, New Jersey, on October 31, 1868, Cement Bill came to Golden from Deadwood, South Dakota, in 1900 to work in a smelter.

Following a year of running the blast furnace at the smelter, Cement Bill became interested in cement work. He began working with contractors but eventually branched out on his own and laid many of Golden's sidewalks. The local hardware stores had such a difficult time keeping up with his cement orders that he gained the moniker "Cement Bill." Eventually, he bought cement by the train or carload.

Cobblestone pillars mark the Golden entrance to Denver Mountain Parks and the Lariat Trail.

In 1911, Cement Bill conceived the idea for a road over Lookout Mountain. He received support from Jefferson County as well as Adolph Coors for the road's construction. Charles Boettcher donated the cement for the Lariat Trail. Bill completed the road in 1914, but failing to receive the final $2,500 payment from the Denver Park Commission, he erected a blockade at the base of the road and refused passage to Denver.

In addition to the Lariat Trail, Cement Bill also worked on many bridges, ditch projects, and dams. He received the contract to line the Beaver Brook water storage facilities owned by Golden. While working on the project, he died on May 17, 1945, and his ashes were scattered at Wildcat Point, the end of the Lariat Trail.

A Golden Educator

Gertrude Bell

Nearly everyone has fond memories of a teacher who had a lasting impact on his or her life. One such teacher in Golden, Gertrude Wheeler, taught for forty-three years and had a positive impact on hundreds of young lives. She was born in June 1876 in Golden.

Gertrude Bell attended South School and Golden High School, from which she graduated in 1894. At that time, the University of Northern Colorado at Greeley was the State Normal School, a teacher training site. Bell graduated with a degree from the Normal School in 1897. She was soon hired to teach in Buffalo Creek, southwest of Golden. While there, she married Laurence Bell.

Gertrude Wheeler Bell's graduating class, Golden High School, 1894.

North School class picture, 1926. Gertrude Bell is in the top row, far right.

Returning to Golden in 1907, Bell began teaching at Fairmont School. In June, she started a kindergarten in her mother's home; it is thought to be the first in Golden. Remaining there for a year, Bell moved on to North School, where she taught until 1941 and served as principal for six of those years. She then moved over to the Central School in downtown Golden and taught until her retirement in 1947. Location wasn't the only change for Bell. She had taught sixth grade for most of her career, but at Central she switched to teaching spelling and math.

Bell's philosophy was, "You can't teach if your pupils hate you." During her lifetime, Bell received many honors for her progressive approach to education. In 1916, the State of Colorado awarded Bell a certificate for outstanding educational work. On one occasion, she was honored as "Mrs. Schoolteacher Personified." Students spoke fondly of her as well, recalling how she made learning a pleasure.

The ultimate honor came in 1963 when the new Golden middle school was named for the popular teacher. However, Bell died in September 1963, a little over two months before the school was opened to students. She is buried at the Golden Cemetery.

Conclusion

"Where the West Lives"

Golden's unofficial motto speaks volumes about the town's view of itself. Some view it as a stagnant and unfortunate picture of an era long passed. Others see the motto as a statement of something more—values, hard work, dedication, entrepreneurship, pioneer spirit, hospitality, and all the romantic images that have long been associated with the American West. These values and spirit are exemplified each and every day by the citizens of Golden's present.

The town itself has grown from a tent settlement to a thriving mini-city. Over the nearly 150 years of Golden's history, many have contributed to its continued growth and viability. They have pushed, prodded, fought, and died for the town's betterment. While countless changes, both cosmetic and profound, have taken place, vestiges of early Golden still peek through—whether it is the original façade of an old building, a descendant of one of the founders, or an idea or issue that continues to arise.

We hope you have enjoyed this stroll through Golden's remarkable past. Many people have passed through and left indelible marks on the town. We can only scratch the surface of the history and stories that have shaped the face of modern Golden. The area has been home to massive dinosaurs, the hunting grounds of brave Native peoples on horseback, a business center for visionary men and women, an educational and research lure for scientists, and an outdoor paradise to the recreation-minded. What will the future hold for Golden? How will its face look in twenty years, fifty years, one hundred fifty years? Who is to say? Rest assured, Golden has been a hub for people and animals for thousands of years; chances are great that the spirit, ingenuity, and love demonstrated by the residents here will ensure a bright and productive future for Golden, the town "Where the West Lives."

A glance down Clear Creek offers a glimpse into Golden's historic past and a view of Golden's promising future ca. 1999.

Bibliography

Books

Abbott, Dan. *One Hundred Years and Counting: The History of Golden, Colorado's Volunteer Fire Department*. Golden, Colo.: D. A. Larsen Consultants, Inc., 1990.

Athearn, Robert. *The Coloradans*. Albuquerque, N.M.: University of New Mexico Press, 1976.

Bancroft, Hubert H. *The Works of Hubert H. Bancroft, Vol. XXV: History of Nevada, Colorado, and Wyoming, 1540–1888*. San Francisco: History Company Publishers, 1890.

Banham, Russ. *Coors: A Rocky Mountain Legend*. Lyme, Conn.: Greenwich Publishing Group, Inc., 1998.

Baskin, O. L. *History of Clear Creek and Boulder Valleys, Colorado*. Chicago: O. L. Baskin and Company Historical Publishers, 1880.

Benson, Maxine, ed. *From Pittsburgh to the Rocky Mountains: Major Stephen Long's Expedition, 1819–1820*. Golden, Colo.: Fulcrum Publishing, 1988.

Berthoud, Edward L. *"History of Jefferson County from 1712 On," WPA History of Jefferson County*, WPA Project #3548. Lakewood, Colo.: Foothills Genealogical Society, 1993.

Black, Robert C. *Railroad Pathfinder: The Life and Times of Edward L. Berthoud*. Evergreen, Colo.: Cordillera Press, 1988.

Bolyrad, Dudley and Stephen Sonnenberg, eds. *Geologic History of the Colorado Front Range*. Denver: Rocky Mountain Association of Geologists, 1997.

Burt, Silas. W. and Edward Berthoud. *The Rocky Mountain Gold Regions: Containing Sketches of Its History, Geography, Botany, Geology, Mineralogy, and Gold Mines*. Denver City, Colo.: Rocky Mountain News Printing Company, 1861.

Butler, G. Montague. *The Clays of Eastern Colorado*. Denver: Smith-Brooks Printing Company, 1915.

Byers, William N. *Encyclopedia of Biography of Colorado: A History of Colorado*. Chicago: Century Publishing and Engraving Company, 1901.

Cassells, E. Steve. *The Archaeology of Colorado*. Boulder, Colo.: Johnson Books, 1997.

Child, Greg. *Climbing: The Complete Reference*. New York City: Facts on File, Inc., 1995.

Citizens Guide to Rocky Flats: Colorado's Nuclear Bomb Factory. Boulder, Colo.: Rocky Mountain Peace Center, 1992.

Corbitt, Thomas B. *The Colorado Directory of Mines*. Denver: Rocky Mountain News Printing Co., 1879.

Craig, Katherine. *Craig's Brief History of Colorado*. Denver: Welch-Haffner Printing Company, 1923.

Crofutt, George. *Crofutt's Grip-Sack Guide of Colorado, Vol.II*. Omaha, Neb.: Overland Publishing Company, 1885.

D'Azevedo, Warren, ed. *Handbook of North American Indians: Great Basin, Vol. 11*. Washington, D.C.: Smithsonian Institution, 1986.

Davis, Leslie B. and Brian O. Reeves, eds. *Hunters of the Recent Past*. London: Unwin Hyman Ltd., 1990.

DeMallie, Raymond J., ed. *Handbook of North American Indians: Plains, Vol. 13 Parts 1, 2*. Washington, D.C.: Smithsonian Institution, 2001.

Fay, Abbott. *Famous Coloradans*. Paonia, Colo.: Mountaintop Books, 1990.

Florence Caldwell Centennial Celebration Committee. *A Century of Women at Mines*. Golden, Colo.: Colorado School of Mines, 1999.

Friesen, John W. *First Nations of the Plains: Creative, Adaptable, and Enduring*. Calgary, Alberta, Canada: Detselig Enterpries Ltd., 1999.

Fuller, Harlin and LeRoy Hafen, eds. *The Journal of Captain John R. Bell: Official Journalist for the Stephen H. Long Expedition to the Rocky Mountains, 1820*. Glendale, Calif.: Arthur H. Clark, 1957.

Gilmore, Kevin P. et al. *Colorado Prehistory: A Context for the Platte River Basin*. Denver: Colorado Council of Professional Archaeologists, 1999.

Hafen, LeRoy, ed. *Colorado Gold Rush: Contemporary Letters & Reports, 1858–1859*. Glendale, Calif.: Arthur H. Clark Company, 1941.

Hoebel, E. Adamson. *The Cheyennes: Indians of the Great Plains*. New York: Harcourt Brace College Publishers, 1978.

Hollister, Ovando. *The Mines of Colorado*. Springfield, Mass.: Samuel Bowles and Company, 1867.

Johnson, Kirk and Robert Raynolds. *Ancient Denver: Scenes from the Past 300 Million Years of the Colorado Front Range*. Denver: DMNS Press, 2001.

Kilburn, Paul D. and Sally White. *North Table Mountain: Its History and Natural Features*. Morrison, Colo.: Jefferson County Nature Association, 1992.

Kohl, Michael and John S. McIntosh, eds. *Discovering Dinosaurs in the Old West: The Field Journals of Arthur Lakes*. Washington, D.C.: Smithsonian Institution Press, 1997.

Kostka, William. *The Pre-Prohibition History of Adolph Coors Company, 1873–1933*. Golden, Colo.: Adolph Coors Co., 1973.

Lakes, Arthur. *Geology of Colorado and Western Ore Deposits*. Denver: The Chain and Hardy Co., 1893.

Lockley, Martin and Lori Marquardt. *A Field Guide to Dinosaur Ridge*. Morrison, Colo.: Friends of Dinosaur Ridge, 1995.

Mehls, Stephen F. *The New Empire of the Rockies: A History of Northeast Colorado*. Denver, Colo.; Bureau of Land Management, 1984.

Morgan, Jesse. *A World School: the Colorado School of Mines*. Denver: Sage Books, 1955.

Nankivel, Major John H. *History of the Military Organizations of the State of Colorado: 1860–1935*. Denver: W. H. Kister Stationery Co., 1935.

Newhouse, Elizabeth, ed. *The Story of America*. Washington, D.C.: National Geographic Society, 1992.

Paterek, Josephine. *Encyclopedia of American Indian Costume*. New York: W. W. Norton & Co., 1994.

Pearl, Richard M. *Colorado Rocks, Minerals, and Fossils*. Denver: Sage Books, 1964.

Ramstetter, Mary. *John Gregory Country*. Golden, Colo.: C Lazy Three Press, 1999.

Richardson, Harold. *Roster of Men and Women Who Served in the World War from Colorado: 1917–1918*. Denver: Colorado National Guard, 1941.

Sage, Rufus B. *His Letters & Papers, 1836–1847, with an annotated reprint of his "Scenes in the Rocky Mountains and in Oregon, California, New Mexico, Texas, and the Grand Prairies," Vol. II*. Glendale, Calif.: Arthur H. Clark, 1956.

Schuller, Gunther. *Early Jazz: Its Roots and Musical Development.* London: Oxford University Press, 1968.

Smith, Duane. *The Birth of Colorado: A Civil War Perspective.* Norman, Okla.: University of Oklahoma, 1989.

Sorgenfrei, Robert. *The Colorado School of Mines: Its Founding and Early Years,* Golden, Colo.: Arthur Lakes Library, Colorado School of Mines, 1999.

Southwell, Carey. *The History of Golden Schools.* Golden, Colo.: Golden Pioneer Museum, 1997.

Strong, Wilbur F., ed. *History of Colorado.* Chicago: S. J. Clarke Publishing Co., 1918.

Taylor, Bayard. *Colorado: A Summer Trip.* Niwot, Colo.: University of Colorado, 1989 (reprint).

U.S. Geological Survey. *Mineral and Water Resources of Colorado.* Washington, D.C.: U.S. Government Printing Office, 1964.

Van Horn, Richard. *Geology of the Golden Quadrangle, Geological Survey Professional Paper #872.* Washington, D.C.: United States Government Printing Office, 1976.

Wagenbach, Lorraine. *St. Joseph's Red Brick Church.* Golden, Colo.: Cimarron Design, 1999.

Wagenbach, Lorraine and Jo Ann Thistlewood. *Golden: The 19th Century.* Littleton, Colo.: Harbinger House, 1987.

Waldman, Carl. *Atlas of the North American Indian.* New York: Facts on File, 1985.

West, Elliott. *Contested Plains: Indians, Goldseekers, and the Rush to Colorado.* Lawrence, Kan.: University Press of Kansas, 1998.

Whiteside, James. *Colorado: A Sporting History.* Boulder, Colo.: University Press of Colorado, 1999.

Willison, George F. *Here They Dug the Gold.* London: Eyre & Spottiswoode, 1950.

Journals & Articles

Allen, Thomas. "Discussion of Opportunities in the Field of Coal Mining Engineers," *Quarterly of the Colorado School of Mines*, Vol. 45 No, 2B (April 1950): 7–11.

Anonymous. "A Buffalo Bill Timeline," *Colorado Prospector.* Vol. 2 No. 8, nd.

"The Dome of the Continent: Colorado in 1872," *Harper's Monthly*; reprinted by Outbooks, Olympic Valley, Calif. 1977.

"The Foothills Art Center," *The Golden Guide*, May 13, 1980.

Budd, M. R. "Colorado and its School of Mines," *The Colorado School of Mines Magazine.* November 1929 to July 1930.

Cassano, James. "Mechanization of Western Coal Mines," *Quarterly of the Colorado School of Mines*, Vol. 45 No, 2B (April 1950): 13–25.

Charles, I. M. "Coal and Its Future," *Quarterly of the Colorado School of Mines*, Vol. 45 No, 2B (April 1950): 68–73.

East, J. H. "Explosives in the Mining Industry," *Quarterly of the Colorado School of Mines*, Vol. 45 No, 2B (April 1950): 341–57.

Eldridge, George Homans. "On Certain Peculiar Structural Features in the Foothill Region of the Rocky Mountains, near Denver, Colorado," *Bulletin of the Philosophical Society of Washington*, Vol. XI (June 1890): 247–74.

Flanagan, Mike. "Adolph Coors, Master Brewer." *Denver Post Magazine*, June 15, 1986.

Fleming, Roscoe. "Engineers of a Thousand Years." *Rocky Mountain Empire Magazine*, September 25, 1949.

Gardner, Richard. "A History of Calvary Episcopal Church," *Annual Report 1996*. Golden, Colo.: Calvary Episcopal Church, 1996.

Golden Lions Club. "60 Years of Golden Lionism: Highlights of Minutes from the Golden Lions Club, 1943–2003." Golden, Colo.: Lions Roar Committee, 2003.

Grunska, Jerry. "Tracks Make a Big Impression on New Golden Links," *Historically Jeffco*. Vol. 14 No. 23 (2002): 1–5.

Harrington, Daniel. "Safety in the Mining Industry," *Quarterly of the Colorado School of Mines*, Vol. 45 No. 2B (April 1950): 173–275.

Johnson, J. Harlan. "Introduction to the Geology of the Golden Area, Colorado," *Quarterly of the Colorado School of Mines*, Vol. XXIX No. 4 (October 1934): 7–36.

Johnson, J. Harlan. "The Geology of the Golden Area, Colorado," *Quarterly of the Colorado School of Mines*, Vol. XXV No. 3 (July 1930): 1–24.

Kimball, Neil W. "George West," *Colorado Magazine*. Vol. XXVII No. 3. 1950: 198–208.

McCormack, M. L. "Seventy-Five Years of Rock Drill Progress, *Quarterly of the Colorado School of Mines*, Vol. 45 No. 2B (April 1950): 326–37.

Martin, Martha. "The County of Vivian," *Historically Jeffco*, Vol. 14 No. 22 (2001): 14–21.

Nelson, Charles E. "The Archaeology of Hall-Woodland Cave," *Southwestern Lore*, Vol. 33 No. 1 (June 1967).

Olsen, Robert. "Adolph Kuhrs and the Founding of His Brewery," *Historically Jeffco*. 1992.

Reese, Joan. "Two Gentlemen of Note: George Morrison, Paul Whiteman, and Their Jazz," *Colorado Heritage*. No. 2 (1986): 2–13.

Ryland, Charles. "The Energetic Captain Berthoud," *Denver Westerners Monthly Roundup*. Vol. XXI Nos. 9&10 (1965): 3–10.

————— "George West: Some of His Accomplishments," *Denver Westerners Monthly Roundup*. Vol. XXV No. 12 (1969): 3–15.

————— "Golden's Resourceful Merchant," *Denver Westerners Monthly Roundup*. Vol. XXVII No 9 (1972): 3–18.

Simpson, Bill. "A History of Calvary Episcopal Church: 1867–1900," *Historic Preservation Report*, nd.

Van Ness, Meg. "History Beneath the Surface: The Early People of the Foothills," *Historically Jeffco*. Vol. 13 No. 21:200): 10–16.

Van Sant, Joel. "Refractory-Clay Deposits of Colorado," Bureau of Mines Report of Investigations #5553, United States Department of the Interior, 1959.

Wearly, W. L. "Trends of Continuous Coal Mining Under Ground," *Quarterly of the Colorado School of Mines*, Vol. 45 No, 2B (April 1950): 41–56.

Newspapers

Central City Daily Register. Vol. 8 No. 204, March 24, 1870.

The Colorado (Golden) Transcript. Golden, Colo., various editions, 1866–2003.

The Denver Post. Denver, Colo., various editions, 1971–2003.

The Golden Globe. Golden, Colo., various editions, 1881–1892.

Jefferson County Republican. Golden, Colo., various editions 1927–1930.

Rocky Mountain News. Denver, Colo., various editions, 1862–1976.

The Western Mountaineer. Golden City, Colo., various editions 1859–1860.

Manuscript and Archive Collections

A Brief History of Faith Lutheran Church, unpublished MS, nd.

A History of the First Baptist Church, unpublished MS, nd.

Brennecke, Betty. *Fortnightly Club Centennial Program*. Golden, Colorado, 1986.

Castle Rock Mountain Railway and Park, Colorado Historical Society; MSS #791.

Cherry Creek Settlements, Colorado Historical Society; MSS #190.

Dempsey, Alice. *History of St. Joseph's Catholic Church*, unpublished MS, 1977.

Edward L. Berthoud, Colorado Historical Society; MSS #56.

History of the First United Methodist Church, unpublished MS, nd.

Noonan, Catherine. *Christian Action Guild*, unpublished MS, nd.

Orlowski, George. *Biography of John Charles Vivian*. Jefferson County, Colorado, nd.

Our Centennial Year, First Presbyterian Church. Church bulletin, 1970.

Reid, Charles and Fran Osseo-Asare. *A History of Calvary Episcopal Church in Golden*, unpublished MS, 1970.

William Austin Hamilton Loveland Lode Book, Colorado Historical Society; MSS #1594.

Thesis

Kennedy, John J. "Annihilation Beckons: the Origins of the Rocky Flats Nuclear Weapons Plant." Ph.D. dissertation, University of Colorado–Denver, 1991.

Other

Bales, John. Personal Interview November 2001.

Barber, Ada Jo. "History: Golden Library." Jefferson County Public Library, nd.

Colorado Department of Corrections, Website, *www.doc.state.co.us*, 2003.

Colorado Department of Human Services, Division of Youth Corrections, Website, *www.cdhs.state.co.us/dyc*, 2003.

Colorado School of Mines, Website, *www.mines.edu*, 2003.

Department of Energy. *Rocky Flat Environmental Technology Site: Photograph Collection*, Golden, Colo., 1980–2002.

General Laws and Joint Resolutions, Memorials, & Private Acts, Passed at the Second Session of the Legislative Assembly of the Territory of Colorado. Denver: Rocky Mountain News Printing Company, 1862.

Golden High School, Website, *www.goldenhighschool.com*, 2003.

Jennings, Cynthia. *Millikin Family History Files*. Unpublished, nd.

Kalasz, Stephen and William Lane Shields. Report of 1994/1996 *Grid Block Archaeological Excavations at the Magic Mountain Site (5JF223) in Jefferson County, Colorado*. Prepared for Colorado Historical Society, State Historic Fund, Project #96–01–049. July 1997.

Morrison Jr., George. Personal Interview 2002.

My Weigh. History of the Pocket Scale, Website, *www.goodscale.com/Historyofthepocketscale.html*, 2004.

National Earthquake Center, Website, *www.neic.cr.usgs.gov*, 2003.

National Renewable Energy Laboratory, Website, *www.NREL.gov*, 2003.

Ordinances of the Town of Golden, complied by H. N. Sales, Town Attorney. Golden, Colo.: Transcript Office, 1877.

Ordinances of the Town of Golden, in Force on the 17th Day of November, 1881. Golden, Colo.: Golden Globe Water Power Print, 1881.

Parfet, William G. "Chip." Personal Interview April 19, 2003.

Private Acts, Joint Resolutions, & Memorials, Passed at the Seventh Session of the Legislative Assembly of the Colorado Territory. Central City: Miner's Register Office, 1868.

Steighorst, Junann. "Mt. Lookout Chapter NSDAR Recalls 60 Years of Outstanding Accomplishments," *History of Mt. Lookout Chapter NSDAR, 1923–1983*. Golden, Colo.: Mt. Lookout Chapter NSDAR, 1983.

Various doc 11/22/04

Index

Documents and compiled references in the archives of the Golden Pioneer Museum.

About the Authors

Michelle Zupan

Michelle Zupan served as the curator of the Golden Pioneer Museum from 2000-2004. She was raised in Northern Virginia, fostering an early passion for all things prehistoric and historic. Michelle holds a B.A. degree with honors in anthropology, with an emphasis in Plains archaeology, from the University of Colorado at Colorado Springs. She has an ABT master's degree from Colorado State University, also in anthropology, with an emphasis in Great Basin archaeology. Her museum training was acquired at the University of Denver. Michelle has worked for several museums since shifting her focus from archaeological fieldwork to museum collections. She served as the NAGPRA collections assistant at both the Denver Museum of Natural History and the Lab for Public Archaeology. She served as both the assistant curator and the interim curator for the Estes Park Historical Museum. In addition, she served as the registrar for the Roswell Museum and Art Center in New Mexico.

Michelle is a volunteer Health and Safety instructor for the American Red Cross, and likes to pursue her favorite hobbies of scuba diving, downhill skiing, fencing, hiking, and cooking. Michelle extends a special thank you to her family and her best pals for all of the support, encouragement, and chocolate provided during the process.

Elinor Packard

Elinor Packard was born in San Diego, California, where she resided for more than forty years. She attended Whitworth College in Spokane, Washington, pursuing a degree in history. Elinor has been married for thirty years and has three grown sons. A ten-year resident of Colorado, she has been the executive director of the Golden Pioneer Museum since November of 1994.

A lifelong interest in history has shaped her life; she gave her first tour of a historic site at the age of sixteen. While her children were still young, she volunteered in Old Town San Diego State Historic Park, where she served on the Board of Directors of the Boosters of Old Town, a nonprofit fundraising and volunteer organization. Since moving to Colorado, she has also served as the vice president of the Association of Northern Front Range Museums, treasurer and president of Golden Cultural Alliance, as a Board member for the Colorado Wyoming Association of Museums, and has volunteered at several area museums. She continues to be passionate about sharing history and preserving our cultural heritage.

About the Photographer

Dave Shrum

Dave Shrum was born in 1936. He developed an interest in photography in junior high school and was photographer for his high school newspaper and yearbook. He worked in a photo lab during high school. He later joined the Air National Guard in 1954, where he was a photographer through 1963. Dave and his father started a photo lab and camera store in 1957, which is now known as Colorado Camera Imaging Center and is the oldest such establishment in the Denver Metro area.